D1289969

Celebrating
Anger

Canadian Cataloguing in Publication Data

The author of this book does not dispense medical advice nor prescribe the use of any technique as a form of treatment for physical, emotional, or medical problems without the advice of a physician. The intent of the author is to offer general information that can help you help yourself. In the event that you use any information in this book for yourself, the author and publisher assume no responsibility for your actions.

Inquiries should be addressed to:
Celebrating Anger
Performance Plus Publishing
2693 Lakeshore Boulevard West, Suite 11
Toronto, Ontario, Canada M8V 1G6

Jackson, Angela Jude, 1940-
Celebrating Anger: Creative Solutions for Managing Conflict

Includes bibliographical references.
ISBN 0-9696836-0-X

1. Anger 2. Self-help Techniques 3. Conflict Management I. Title

BF575A5J3 1993   152.4'7   C93-093221-8

The Production Team

Cover design and layout:	Kathleen Brindley
Typesetting:	Bindernagel-Ross
Illustrations:	Samantha Andrew
Photo:	Glamour Shots
Printing:	Webcom

Celebrating Anger

by Angela Jackson

Performance Plus Publishing
Toronto, Ontario, Canada

Acknowledgements

I would like to acknowledge the following:

My Higher Power who guides me with a loving hand.

The 12-Step programs and the people who carry the message of these programs. My deepest gratitude and love.

Yogi Amrit Desai and the Kripalu family, who taught me that the spiritual path is a celebration.

My father who told me I could be anything I wanted, and my mother who taught me "If at first you don't succeed, try, try again."

My children Tanya, Cybele, and Damion, who have always been my greatest teachers. Who have loved me when I was unable to love myself, and who have helped me accept myself as I am.

My husband Fraser, who urged me to write this book and then stayed out of my way when I did. Thank you for the meals, the massages, and your love.

My special National Speakers Association friends who read the manuscript and offered suggestions and encouragement: in particular, Reva Nelson, Sue Jewell and Steve Schklar. Thanks also to Rosalie Wysocki, who encouraged me by promising to buy the first case of books.

I also want to thank Kathleen Brindley, who designed the cover and worked on page layout; Samantha Andrews for her drawings; Cliff Luis for his sensitive editing; and Susan Bindernagel, of Bindernagel-Ross, who did a superb job of typesetting.

And you, dear reader. Without you, there would be no reason to write.

Dedication

This book is dedicated to every person who has attended my seminars, and to anyone who has difficulty with anger and is willing to make positive life changes.

TABLE OF CONTENTS

Preface

The Power of Anger

"I get so angry, I feel like hitting someone."

"I don't get angry but I do get depressed."

"Expressing anger feels unnatural."

"When I get angry I become obsessed with vengeful thoughts."

"I don't get angry, I get even."

Do you ever feel like this?

Could these be your words?

ANGER. We all have it! That's what makes it such a fascinating subject.

It doesn't matter who you are, what your title or job, or how your financial statement reads, you too have been angry. And

1

why not? It's a perfectly legitimate and profoundly human emotion.

So why do we get into so much trouble with it, and how can we make it work for us instead of against us?

The answer to these questions form the basis of this book.

Anger is anger is anger. Like a sleeping cat, anger lies curled within us, ready to spring into action, often when we least expect it.

Anger is always within us and it always will be. It is part of our make-up, our built-in survival mechanism. That's why it is so important to acknowledge our anger, to take it out of whatever closet we stuff it into and to have a good look at it in the light of day.

We need to understand our anger, so we can turn it into power that works *for* us instead of against us. We need to learn, then use, some effective tools to manage anger, because if we're not managing anger, it's managing us.

This book is about celebrating anger, with all its joys and terrors. It is about understanding the gift our anger can give us in the form of self-recognition. Ultimately this book is about choice — the choice each one of us has of recognizing the enormous power our anger brings us, and of using this power as a creative force in our lives. This is a choice we need to make over and over again, for it is a choice of personal liberation.

Please make this book your own. Turn down page corners, underline, make notes. Write any comments or notations that you want to, for this is your book, to be used in whatever way you choose. If you don't like what I'm saying, and especially if it makes you angry, get a red pen and scratch it out, or use bold markers to draw faces beside the print. The best thing you could do is express your anger with me. See it come alive in whatever form you choose.

We are going on a journey together. I invite you to participate actively and enjoy each step we take. I have included specific exercises that will help you transform anger into creative energy. You will find them liberally sprinkled throughout the book. **PLEASE DO THE EXERCISES**. They are vital to releasing the past and claiming a joyous future. I also suggest that you start an anger journal. You can use an ordinary notebook that you keep with you to track your anger habits. You will find this journal to be an invaluable asset in helping you identify and release old anger patterns.

Chapter One

Qualifying

We shall not cease from exploration
And the end of all our exploring
Will be to arrive where we started
And know that place for the first time.

T.S. Eliot

They call me the anger expert. I'm the one who is brought in when nothing else works. I'm the person you go to see when your relationship is crackling with dynamite and a bomb detonator is needed. Corporations call me when there is a backlog of hostility that is threatening to explode all over the office. I am called whenever people feel resentful and frustrated and don't know what to do. I hope I am called in before the firing squad arrives.

I deal with management groups, sales teams, and front line personnel. I work in elegant hushed offices and noisy factories. I deal with chief executive officers and lead hands. I also work with couples. Again, I hope to get to them before they call their lawyers.

The format my work usually takes is on-site consultation followed by training, reinforced with follow-up.

I'm the expert because I'm a person who's had a lot of anger in life and I've finally learned how to deal with it. I'm someone who has botched up relationships, lost opportunities, hurt myself and others because of anger. I've been a victim, thrown violent temper tantrums, been defiant, willful, reactive, and stubborn. I've been strong-minded and raging.

I've played every anger game

I've been subversive and offensive in my anger output. I've been passive-aggressive, manipulative, conniving, forceful, dominating, a retreater, and a suck. I've played every anger game I later read of, and made up new ones to boot. I've chosen relationships with some of the angriest men I've ever encountered, and lived to write this book.

Clearly, I've made most of the mistakes anyone who is full of anger does. I think that's what being an expert really means: someone who makes plenty of mistakes, and learns from them.

I'm a slow learner. It has taken me a very long time to accept and then manage my anger.

I've earned my anger stripes.

I've paid the price and suffered the consequences. Now I have a good idea of what works and what doesn't.

I have degrees in psychology and education, but my best teachers have been the people with whom I've had relationships. They taught me about my own anger and denial. They helped me become the person I am now.

Today I celebrate anger, much as one celebrates joy, in a spirit of acceptance and delight. I've made friends with my anger. I am amused by it. The best news is that I'm not afraid of anger anymore, and I'm not tyrannized by it either.

During the past 10 years I've specialized in anger and conflict management. I've developed workshops, and deliver both workshops and keynote presentations throughout Canada and the United States.

People write me letters and testimonials about how their lives have changed as a result of these presentations. My goal is *to help people who are willing to make the necessary changes*. The tools I use are effective if used on a continuous basis. I believe that is the best acknowledgement. I have never given a workshop where someone complained or said it was a waste of time. No one has wanted their money back, although I offer a money-back guarantee. I tell you this because the workshops and counselling sessions have a high rate of success. I want you to know that the material you read comes from experience with people. **It can work for you too**.

If you choose to do the work.

That's the qualifier. You have to decide that you want to do the work. You need to make a commitment and count yourself in.

I teach what I need to learn

So, how did such an angry person become a successful speaker, seminar leader, and consultant? The simplest answer is, "I teach what I needed to learn."

I've spent half a century in the anger laboratory, first practising anger, then developing and testing strategies to handle it — strategies that I now pass on to you.

The more lengthy answer is, "By trial and error."

By thinking that nothing would ever work for me and learning, almost in retrospect, that it had. By making a commitment to do the anger work and staying with the commitment, even when my insides were screaming.

Sure, I still trip myself up and get caught. I'm a human being after all. I am not rid of anger; I never will be. The good news is that I am no longer in denial about my anger.

Today, I use it as my teacher and my friend. I have great respect for my anger. It has served me well. It has brought me to you.

This book is a primer on dealing with anger. It contains every strategy I have ever learned, and successfully used, to deal with anger. It has bits of philosophy, case histories, conversations, humour, and a lot of love.

Ultimately it is love that pulls us all through and it is love I offer you throughout this book. Unconditional love, the kind that has enabled me to accept myself as I am. Unconditional love, which also enables me to accept you just the way you are right now, with whatever "warts" you may have.

It's okay if you get annoyed with me at any point in this book.

Feel free to be suspicious or disbelieving. It's okay if you think the strategies will never work for you. I once felt the same way. Just stick with it and keep on reading. Remember, the most expensive thing you will ever own is a closed mind, so keep your mind open when it wants to snap shut.

It doesn't matter if you have past or present resentments, remorse, guilt, denial, or even frozen feelings and inner numbness. It's all okay. All these sensations are grist for the mill, and together we will grind up the chaff and make a fine harvest.

Chapter Two

My Story

I celebrate myself, and sing myself,
And what I assume, you shall assume,
For every atom belonging to me
As good as belongs to you.

Walt Whitman

Yes, it's time to share my story with you. Go get a cup of coffee or tea and make yourself comfortable.

I was the first child born into a middle class family in English Montreal. It was the war year and the atmosphere in Montreal was tense. People lived on rations, women helped in the war effort, and radio news reports were always the topic of conversation.

None of those things I remember

I was a fair-haired pretty child who had a daddy she adored and a mother with whom she locked horns. One of my earliest memories is of being four years old and my mother scrubbing my mouth out with soap for something I said. Then I was taken to a corner of my bedroom and told to stand for an hour so I would learn to behave. Instead, I drew pictures on the wall and was spanked and punished again. This gives you an inkling of my young personality. I didn't care about the impending punishment; I acted out my defiance.

My parents divorced when I was six. My father left town and my mother was left with me and my baby brother. I was sent to innumerable foster homes, some of which I still can't remember. What they had in abundance was abuse — physical, mental, emotional, and sexual. I was slapped, punched, strapped, jeered at, and used as a commodity.

When I was nine I was used sexually by a foster father. Every Wednesday night, when his wife went to bingo, he would come into my room, force me to kneel in front of him, and then shove himself at me. I would wretch and gag, but this didn't deter him. Grabbing me by the hair, he would extract my promise to be silent, threatening to cut off my head if I ever told anyone.

I hated and feared him. I was also enraged. This anger probably saved my sanity, for after a year of surviving those Wednesday nights, I was angry enough to risk getting my head cut off. So I told a girl at school, who told her mother, who told the wife, who called in a Children's Aid worker.

I remember being taken upstairs to the bathroom with my mother and the Children's Aid worker. I sat on the toilet and they stood beside me. They both told me I had to apologize and tell the wife that I had made the whole thing up.

"We know you are lying," said the worker. "You have to go downstairs and apologize, otherwise she'll leave her husband, and that would be terrible. What would happen to their little baby Ralphie? You wouldn't want him to suffer, would you?" I looked at my mother, pleading with my eyes for her to say something, to take my side. She was silent.

I felt as if I was being flushed down the very toilet I sat on. I remember being hot with both anger and shame. I pushed these feelings deep inside me and went downstairs to apologize.

I don't remember what happened after that

I do know that soon after I was packed up and sent to Toronto to live with my father and his new bride. My father was a full-blown alcoholic by this time, totally out of control, but I didn't know it. I adored my father. He was tall, he had flaming red hair, and he told me wonderful stories. Although I was wary of people and didn't make friends with other kids, I was happy for the first time in years.

I rode my bike as if it were a magic steed and built myself a secret fort in the woods, where I would play happily with the little dog my father had bought for me.

My idyll didn't last long. One night I saw my father tiptoe into my room and take my suitcase from the top of the closet. In the morning he was gone. The antique doll my mother had given me and the bike she'd sold her piano to buy for me were also gone. In their place were two blue tickets, pawn tickets that were never cashed in.

Margie, the new wife, kept me for a week and then shipped me back to my mother in Montreal. It was supposed to be my "birthday surprise" visit.

My mother was quick to tell me that in fact I was never going back to Toronto. My father had left again. His new wife was returning to her parents, and she, my mother, was stuck with me. I remember picking up the birthday card Margie had given me. It was a musical cardboard box with a wind-up crank that played "Happy Birthday." I remember playing that song backwards, over and over again. I can still sing that backwards melody today.

It looked and felt like a prison

My mother sent me to what she called a boarding school. It was a three-hour drive from Montreal and it housed about a hundred kids. With iron gates and locks on the outside of the bedroom doors, it looked and felt like a prison to me. I hated being there. I was angry at everyone by now but I didn't understand what anger was, or that I had the right to have it. I was angry and in pain but I shoved those feelings down inside my stomach, and became determined. Every Saturday I would attempt to run away. I'd slit the inner lining of my coat, and during the week I'd smuggle bread and fruit into this coat. It got to be an event. On Saturdays the older kids would lean out of the window to cheer me on, placing bets on how far I'd get.

Every time I ran, I was caught, brought back, strapped, and put into "solitary" — a little green room with a tiny barred window. My time spent in that little room varied depending on whether it was needed more for someone else, but it was always a few days. I didn't like being in solitary, but I was defiant and every so often I'd run away again. One time I made it all the way to Montreal. It was at least 100 miles and it felt like quite an achievement.

I found my mother's apartment in the middle of the city and was convinced that because I'd successfully managed to get there, she'd understand that I was smart, and would now let me live with her. Instead she called the school. I was in solitary for two weeks.

There was no way out for me

I didn't run away after that. I was 11 years old and knew there was no way out for me.

This didn't stop me from provoking the teachers or becoming a class clown. I didn't care about getting my mouth or head slapped. I was used to it. The strap didn't deter me one bit. I was full of rage, and when I couldn't contain it anymore I blasted whoever was in my way. This blasting took the form of calling people names and saying whatever hurtful words came into my mouth. That's the way I started to express my anger and it became a habit for me, one I justified.

I figured I had a right to my anger. After all, my father had red hair and I looked like him. Everyone knew redheads had a temper. Even then, I reasoned to myself that my anger was justified. It was my own personal badge of distinction. It gave me an edge and some notoriety. I didn't know that the reason I was so angry was because of my past and the stored-up feelings I harboured. I thought it was because I was living at that boarding school and couldn't escape. Anger served as a protection from feeling my feelings. I couldn't cry but I could make a quick retort.

At 12 I moved into what was to be my last foster home, where my young brother was also living. Anger was the ruling force in that household too, and I was often the scapegoat. I pretended I was stronger than I was. I stuck my chin up and acted as if I didn't care.

I'd drag her to bed

When I was 13 my mother moved into a two-bedroom apartment, got a roommate, and allowed me to live with her. She'd work by day and drink by night. Often she'd pass out and I'd drag her to bed.

Later in the night she'd wake up, storm into my room, switch on the light, and, with broom in hand, poke me out of bed and force me to clean up the mess I'd made. My mother and I were still at it you see. Only now she was menopausal and I just starting puberty, so both of our emotional states were heightened. We seemed to be locked into a game of anger, which we played with great intensity. I'd leave my clothes on the floor. She'd say nothing when she came home from work, then she'd burst into midnight action with her broom. My mother suppressed her feelings. Then she'd drink to get some relief, which allowed her to act out her rage. It was a no-win situation for both of us and my anger mounted.

That same year I heard that my father died of cirrhosis of the liver — whatever that meant — and I also discovered booze in my mother's bureau drawer. Rye whiskey.

I hated the smell and the taste of rye, so I held my nose and drank it. I was curious to see why my mother liked it so much.

It didn't take long to find out. It was wonderful. I loved the feeling, the wonderful warm feeling of the booze hitting the empty pit of my stomach, immediately coating it with a fuzzy sensation. It was love at first thud. Instant attraction.

I sure hated being me

I can still remember the moment of freedom I had with that first slug of rye. It was freedom from deep pain I didn't know I held.

Freedom from worry, from anger, from just being me — and I sure hated being me. I believe my own alcoholism was born in that first drinking experience but I was only 13 then, and had years to go before admitting it.

Drinking fortified me, gave me courage, helped ease my burdens. When booze didn't work to keep away the night terrors, my mother's pills, Seconal and Valium, did. Of course, I didn't drink too much in those early teenage years, but every time I did, it was to get drunk and inwardly escape.

I grew older. I was good-looking, smart, and a daredevil. I was also a virgin, because I believed that kept me special, until one night a boy I hardly knew locked me in a room, held me captive, and ended that specialness.

I was full of shame

I was 16 and I figured I had a lot to be angry at. I hated authority figures, my mother, men, and, most of all, myself. I changed my name. My name was Jude until then, and I was full of shame about being me, so instead I took the name Angela, because my father had often called me his angel.

At 20 I married a young German I met in a bar. Together we fought, drank, and had babies. Then we fought some more. The fights grew worse. At first I was the victim and he the perpetrator. Then one time he came after me and I grabbed a knife for protection. Wonder of wonders, I saw fear in my husband's eyes and, for the first time, I felt the thrill of violent power. Now my husband and I began a new step in our dance of danger.

I became the tormentor. I would demean him, laugh at him, and send him derogatory glances. In my husband I saw all the people who had hurt me. I projected them upon him and saw him as the enemy. We spent 11 years together, locked in an angry alliance. The one vow we both held onto was fidelity. I broke this vow and took a young lover.

My husband reacted like a wounded bull, raging and attempting to beat up my lover, raging and threatening to take the children away from me. I retaliated by telling him our youngest son wasn't his, an outright lie, but one I knew would hurt him. By now I was numb. I didn't care whom I hurt or why. I drank my worries and pain away. I drank my guilt down. I drank to keep the spark of love aglow with my young lover.

I started a new life. I had a new relationship, a career, and my three kids. Everything was going well, but there was a time bomb ticking away inside of me. For a while things were good with the young lover, but then I started to boss him around and discovered I preferred that role. It made me feel strong. I became a bully, masterful at verbal abuse, knowing exactly how to twist the knife. I became so good at it that he left.

I was in deep trouble

Now my three children bore the brunt of my rage. I would alternately kiss and hit them. They never knew what to expect.

By day I worked. At night I fuelled my anger with booze and suppressed my pain with Valium and barbituates. I was acting just like the mother I'd despised, but I couldn't see it. I had no idea that I was angry. I was in deep trouble. I was suicidal and depressed. I'm sure I would have died had I not experienced the following moment of truth.

It was on one of those ordinary evenings, when I was coming up the basement stairs with another bottle of wine so that I could "unwind." As I entered the kitchen I saw my 13-year-old daughter staring at me with a look of total disgust. I recognized that look. It was the same one I had felt for my mother. In that split second I saw myself as I really was. In a state of shock I realized I had a big problem and needed help. I made a telephone call and found a 12-step program that was tailor-made for me.

I began to live

I was 39 and praying for death. Instead I began to live. My self-help group became my family and my school. I could talk about my atheism and mistrust. No one shut me up. I didn't have to please anyone. I could simply be me, and be accepted. This unconditional acceptance probably saved my life. I couldn't cry — that was for weaklings — but I could talk. Gradually the inner loneliness began to abate as I worked the 12 steps. I started to become aware of my feelings. I also went for therapy. Slowly I began to change my behaviour with my children, to open up to life again.

I went on dates and got involved with another angry man. He'd spew his venom and I'd cower and try to distract him, much as I had initially done with my husband. Gradually I began to realize that his anger was a reflection of my own. I had buried my anger, and deceived myself about it. I believed my anger only came out when I was provoked; therefore, it was legitimate and not my fault. Other people were the problem. They provoked me so much that I couldn't handle it!

Denial was my problem

Denial was what my problem really was. I had to come to terms with the fact that I was fully responsible for how I acted and reacted. It took me a long time to see that I was acting like a victim, that I had felt like a victim ever since that first foster home. I had to *see* before I could begin to change. Then slowly I realized that the angry man I had chosen was a *mirror* of my own buried feelings.

19

I had deliberately picked angry men because, on a level I couldn't see, I felt at home with them. I understood their ferocity. It was familiar. It was like my own. As I began to *see* what I was doing, I also began to change.

I started noticing the feeling of anger in my stomach; just noticing when it would appear, without my having to act on it. This was difficult because when I reacted I didn't have to feel anything. I could just spout off. Now I began to *feel* my feelings, which were often painful. I had never allowed myself to feel my authentic feelings, so this was very new.

I taught myself to observe other people's anger — to simply observe what I saw without having to rescue them from it, or quiet them down, or run away. I discovered I was terrified of anger. I thought the anger I saw or felt was so ferocious it would never subside. Like a giant ink blot, I thought it would keep on growing until it annihilated everyone and everything in its wake. I started to breathe deeply instead of reacting with fear, and the breathing allowed me space to observe.

Gradually I was able to let this fear of anger subside.

I no longer needed an angry relationship to wage war in, but I didn't know how to have a healthy one either, so I had none.

I needed to do a lot of work

I spent the next few years living with my children, not dating, working on myself, and on my reactions and habits. I needed to do a lot of work on me. I read every book that was relevant, and practised what I learned. I went to workshops and retreats. I wanted desperately to stop being my own worst enemy. I continued going to my self-help group and to work the 12 steps. I changed my habits. I stopped smoking and began exercising. I investigated nutrition and developed a healthy diet. I worked with my own arthritis. I took charge of my life.

My persistence paid off. I began to experience an inner peace I had only glimpsed before. It was no longer necessary for me to create drama or crisis in order to avoid my feelings. I could now identify what I was feeling and discern that usually I was triggered by something from my past, which I would then act out in the present. I got better at controlling my reactions. There were still angry flare-ups, but I had developed tools to neutralize these explosions.

Finally, it became important for me to get inside the scabs — the pain beneath the anger. I had to feel the painful feelings of rejection and abandonment I'd stifled so many years before. I had to own the pain, then grieve my losses and experience the wounds before I could let them go and be healed. This all took time. Over the years I developed a deeper understanding of the power of anger. I knew how it felt to repress it and express it. I understood what lay behind anger, and finally I could deal with it.

Anger became my trusted friend

No longer was I afraid of anger, mine or anyone else's. I was no longer a victim. I was truly able to turn anger around in my own life and to make it my ally. Now when I became instantly enraged I knew it was a signal for me to go deeper, to figure out where the original fear or pain came from. Anger became my trusted friend. It was anger, after all, that had kept me surviving, had kept me going during those long hard years, and had given me fuel for living. Anger had helped me hide when I was too afraid to look at myself, and when I did look, anger led me to the next step of my journey. It was anger that told me there was something deeper going on inside me, and that I was generally resorting to unconscious behaviour to avoid really seeing myself. Anger led me to my hidden pain, and once I learned

21

to release the pain, I could feel an expansive inner lightness — and then exuberance — that invariably followed.

Anger is a profound teacher

I learned what a profound teacher anger was. I asked myself, "What if I could take this anger power and channel it into creativity? What would happen in my own life, in other's lives?"

I went to work on it. I developed anger strategies and started giving anger workshops, initially at the high school level, working with rebellious teenagers. Those teenagers taught me a lot. They had anger issues that made me feel like Miss Muffet. I worked for eight years in a tough inner-city high school, developing and refining a conflict management program, seeing the changes my students were able to make and to keep on making. Watching them use their anger as a catalyst for change, I knew I was onto a method so powerful it could change lives.

I began giving anger management workshops to teachers and principals in the education system, and discovered the demand was so great and the work so relevant that it could help people in any field. I took my program to other workplaces, and have done so ever since.

Today my life works

I keep on learning, refining, practising, and sharing what I learn. I have a university degree, but it's not in anger. I believe my own experience is my degree. I've paid my dues.

Eventually I married again, and today have a loving, supportive relationship. Today my life works. My children are grown up now. They are beautiful people, and I am proud of each one. Of course they have baggage and scars to heal, and each is grappling with his/her issues in a different way. My eldest daughter is like quicksilver. She is organized, speedy, bright, and super-responsible. She looks after everyone but neglects herself. Recently she developed epilepsy and has to slow down. She has joined a self-help group and is consciously allowing herself to relax more in life.

My second daughter (the 13-year-old who gave me my moment of truth) is a sensitive beauty and a talented actress. She is both witty and intelligent, and she also experiences bouts of depression. She has now decided to investigate the nature of this malady and get to its roots.

My youngest child, my son, has just begun his independent journey. He is studying theatre in B.C. and is excited with what he is learning. He is a kind and caring fellow, yet he also grapples with some self-destructive tendencies.

I think every one of us has some area in life that needs to be healed. My children are no exception. I believe they will find the support and love they need to help them. If I could live my parenting years over, of course I would do it differently. I have had to learn to accept my mistakes, to accept the past, and let it go. What amazes me, and what I am truly grateful for, is the love my children have given and continue to give to me. We share our experiences together. We talk openly about our lives. There is a ready acceptance between us. I treasure the emotional honesty my children share with me, and I am deeply grateful that I was able to get the help I needed so that I can be available to them today.

Your Story

Your story is different, of course. You may have had a worse or a better time of it. My husband, for example, was never beaten or abandoned as a child, but he was ignored and criticized. His anger took a different form. He became a depressive, turning his anger in on himself. Although he is an intelligent man, he practised failure, first in school and later in life, sabotaging any successes he might have had. Always a "nice" guy, he is supportive of other people, a great listener, a good friend. However, he lived a minimal existence for many years, using television to anaesthetize his feelings.

By doing the anger work, he was able to identify and transform his anger, to use it as a life signal — a turn-around vehicle. As a result, today he has the energy he needs to make his life work. Today he is a free man, successful in his own eyes, confident of his abilities and able to make a contribution to others.

Whatever your anger situation is, you can change it, if you choose to. You can pick up the tools that this book will provide, and use them to make the difference.

I know you can do it. All that is required is your desire to do the work, and your time. You will make mistakes, but that's part of the process. You will grow, and you will learn to love yourself. That's the other part of the process. Be patient with yourself. Do only what feels right for you at any given moment and then stop. Go at your own speed and give yourself permission for "time out."

Do the exercises in each chapter. They are very important and will help you take charge of your life.

I invite you to start with the exercise on the next page.

EXERCISE ONE
My Anger Story

You can begin to write your anger story here.

Let it come out, just the way it is.

Go back to when you were little and write about what hurt you and what made you mad. Try not to edit or judge. Don't worry about grammar or spelling, if those are issues for you. Simply write out your feelings. Write out the way it was for you. This is your opportunity to purge, to get it all out.

Take as much time as you need. Begin now if you can, then block off more time later. Make sure you don't avoid this exercise for it is crucial to your own self-knowledge and to getting the most out of this book and your own life.

Allow yourself to feel your feelings as you write. Accept that this is how it has been for you. Then pick up this book and continue your journey with me.

My Anger Story

I want you to know that I care about you and I understand your suffering. That's why I have written this book. You are not alone in your feelings of hatred, envy, pride, guilt, fear, remorse, or denial. You have a right to your feelings. You have a right to feel angry. Acknowledge this fact. Then, when you are ready, you can move on to the next step.

EXERCISE TWO
Examining Anger Patterns

Look over your anger story and pick out some of your major resentments. Make a list of what made you angry when you were little, and also look at your reactions and how you behaved at the time. Write this all down.

Once you have written out a list of your past behaviour, check to see if you still use that same behaviour pattern today. I've included two examples that might be helpful in your own examination.

Example 1:

Fact

When I was little, I was angry because my father didn't come home often.

Behaviour

I had temper tantrums and took my anger out on my mother.

Today

I still have temper tantrums and take my anger out on people I love.

Example 2:

Fact

I was the youngest of four children and I didn't get a lot of attention. This made me angry.

Behaviour

I used to imagine myself playing with lots of kids and having a different family.

Today

I still daydream and watch T.V. a lot. I guess I spend a fair bit of time fantasizing.

Now it's your turn. Take some time and write out your list of "Fact," "Behaviour," and "Today." Think of at least three examples so you can track your patterns.

Fact

Behaviour

Today

Angela Jackson

Fact

Behaviour

Today

Fact

Behaviour

Today

Do you see any patterns? Are you still reacting and behaving in ways that were a response to the pain you felt in your childhood, but which are not helpful to you today? Would you like to change any of these habits? You can, if you choose to.

Start with your imagination. Einstein said, "Imagination is more important that knowledge." Visualize yourself taking your collection of facts and behaviours and stuffing it all into a giant, thick garbage bag.

Then visualize yourself loading the bag into an imaginary truck and driving to the garbage dump. See yourself dumping this inner garbage at the dump, and feel the freedom you experience. Notice the feeling; allow it to remain with you.

Anchor this experience in your body by clapping your hands or touching a part of you, for example your right elbow. This will remind you of your ability to dump your own garbage. In fact, you can use this system anytime you want to release old resentments. You don't have to keep repeating old patterns of behaviour. You don't have to harbour grudges. You can truly let them go. Of course, if you miss having those resentments you can always go to the dump and get them back.

By doing this work you have already taken a giant step in changing your life and your attitude. Give yourself a pat on the back. You deserve it! Acknowledge your own achievement. Believe in the work you have done. You will experience a new sense of freedom and peace, and I invite you to give yourself plenty of time to take this in.

Chapter Three

How the Trouble Begins

*You cannot escape from a prison
if you don't know you are in one.*

Vernon Howard

Anger is neither good nor bad. Most of us have a tendency to believe that anger is sometimes good because it gets things off our chest. We also tend to believe that anger is mostly bad because we feel it so strongly.

Women, in particular, often believe anger is bad, especially their own. We've been brought up to be good girls, to be "sugar and spice and all things nice." Although we know this is a tall order, we feel guilty if we even feel anger, let alone express it. Good girls don't show anger. Bitches do, and who wants to don that label? So we hide our anger; repress it; suppress it. Eventually we either get sick from it or sick of it, and all hell breaks loose.

We've all read stories of men who were loners or quiet all their lives until suddenly they went crazy and gunned down their family or someone else's. We don't often hear about women doing this because women usually hurt themselves. Here are three examples of women who did just that.

LILA

Lila had a lot of suppressed anger. She was taught that children should be seen and not heard, and that nice girls weren't supposed to show anger, ever.

Lila was a nice girl. Nonetheless, she had a lot to be angry about. When she was a teenager, Lila lost her entire family in a fire. She became emotionally numb because of this terrible accident, but she kept a "stiff upper lip." On the outside she appeared "normal."

She moved in with a maiden aunt until she could finish high school and get a job. Lila was talented. She was artistic: she could draw and paint. However, it was 1932 and there was no money for her to pursue her talents. She got an office job. Subsequently, she met a man and got married.

Lila had three miscarriages before giving birth to her first child. She wanted the child to be a boy because that's what her husband wanted. Instead, she had a girl. Five years later she had a boy, but her husband ran off with a young beauty queen when the boy was a year old, leaving Lila penniless.

In 1945 jobs were scarce and money was tight. Lila got a job as a salesgirl, but she couldn't afford to keep her children so she put them in foster homes and rented herself a room. Lila did the best she could in these circumstances. She visited her kids on alternate weekends and tried to cope with her own depression. But things kept getting worse. Her daughter was molested. Her son lost his arm in an accident. And no handsome, rich stranger materialized to rescue any of them.

Lila was angry but she never expressed it. She had an inner trunk full of pain but she couldn't share it. She wouldn't cry or yell. She had been taught to "smile and the world smiles with you." Even though there was no evidence of a world smiling with her, Lila put on her smiling face. As for her feelings, well, at night she began taking a drink or two, just to get rid of the tension she felt. She drank to ease the loneliness and the hurt.

Lila did have girlfriends with whom she chatted. She was a good friend, and a good listener. You could tell your troubles to Lila and know you would find a sympathetic ear. Clearly, she knew what troubles were herself.

Years went by. Finally, Lila met a man who could offer her some companionship. They went to movies. They played bridge. They took trips, although they always stayed in separate bedrooms. There was no physical relationship but Lila didn't complain. She took what she could get. They didn't live together but they talked every night on the telephone, and she always had a Saturday night date.

Lila worked in an office until she was 62. Then she had a stroke, caused, the doctor said, by her drinking. She was hospitalized for a year and gradually recuperated. Once she was out of the hospital, Lila returned home to her dark little apartment, and began drinking again. She drank to avoid her feelings. Her children had grown up, moved away, married, then divorced. Neither one was really involved in Lila's life but she never complained or asked for more. She had a few friends and her bottles for consolation.

When she was 70, Lila moved to a different province at her companion's request. She didn't want to move. She was very attached to her apartment and to her city. She'd never wanted to live anywhere else, but he wanted to be near what remained of his family. On arriving, he found an apartment for himself and a retirement home for Lila. Two months later he died. There she was, alone in a strange place, her furniture gone and her dearest friend departed.

Lila moved from that retirement home to another and then another, looking for the right one, but never finding it. In the process she broke her hip. She had an operation that failed, which led to another operation. She finally ended up in a nursing home. She hated it. Although she had money stashed away, she wouldn't spend it on herself. She wanted to leave it to her children. She stayed in the nursing home and began complaining. Lila also had arthritis. Her arms ached. Her fingers curled into tight little fists. She took pills for arthritis, pills to sleep at night, and pills for the seizures she had after her stroke. She got madder and madder about her life. These were the golden years she had been looking forward to, yet here she was stuck in a nursing home, alone, with few visitors and no friends.

Then, in a smoking accident, she burned her chest badly — so badly that she had to have a large skin graft. The new skin didn't stretch enough so she couldn't raise her head very high. The pain was terrible. It was as if she was burning alone in that fire that had claimed her family so many years before, as if she were still doing penance for having survived the fire.

For the first time Lila expressed anger. The anger that she had stored for a lifetime began to be emerge. Sure, along the way she had had an occasional outburst, but those had been few and far between. Now she gave up on God and on decorum. She let her anger rip. She started to scream at the staff. She would throw her food on the floor and call the nurses names. When the aides would try to dress her and would inadvertently touch her burned flesh, Lila would scratch and bite. As a result she was sedated, put in a wheelchair, and stuck in a corner. Lila had become "a bad girl."

Her body was in perpetual pain. She couldn't be taken outdoors in the wheelchair because she would scream with the pain. Most of the time she raged and swore — she, who had always been a perfect lady with eloquent diction and impeccable vocabulary. She glared. She sneered. The resulting expression looked demonic. Yet she was perfectly sane, lucid, and quite aware of what she was doing and saying.

She simply could not contain her anger any longer. The inner trunk, which she used for storage, had burst open and the anger rushed out. It was as if all the rage and pain that she had held in her life erupted at once, out of control. But she wouldn't see a therapist, she couldn't connect with her emerging feelings, and she didn't get relief. Last year Lila died in the nursing home. At dinner one evening her head plopped onto her plate and that was it. The end of a life.

LIZ

Liz was 50 when she developed breast cancer. Poor Liz. She was such a good person, so kind. She was a nurse. She cared for people all her life, but she never truly cared for herself. Liz had never married. She had some unpleasant experiences with men, and she preferred the company of her women friends. She loved her profession. She wove beautiful tapestries in her spare time. She was well-travelled, well-read, and financially secure.

Liz had never exhibited anger about any aspect of her life. She withdrew from any sort of conflict or confrontation. She did occasionally clench her teeth, especially when she talked about her parents or brother. Her brother was sickly and, in her opinion, had always taken more than his share of attention. This was the one area that she would begin to get worked up about, but she would quickly drop the subject, and stifle those feelings. "No use crying over spilled milk," she'd say. Liz was a friend to everyone, a positive thinker, and a giver in life.

When she developed her first tumour, she was nursing full-time and taking care of her mother in the evenings. She decided to fight her cancer. She gave up her job, had an operation, took chemotherapy, changed her diet, and immersed herself in books about cancer. She couldn't verbally express her anger, but she did stop visiting her brother. She made quick progress with her illness and within a year was given a clean bill of health.

Liz then took a six-month trip to Spain. She returned home to find her mother's health had deteriorated and she was now bed-ridden. Liz moved in with her mother and nursed her day and night.

Within two months Liz developed headaches and discovered that she had a brain tumour, which was inoperable. Liz died the following spring. Her mother is doing well.

WANDA

Then there was Wanda, who died of a tumour when she was 32.

Wanda was a researcher. She was quiet, well-mannered, and kind. She went to church regularly. She was engaged and was busy planning her wedding when she went for her regular physical checkup. Wanda's doctor suggested that she have the mole on her bikini line removed. It was a simple procedure, so Wanda decided to do it. Within two months of the operation, Wanda developed a malignant tumour where the mole had been. It grew to the size of a melon. Four weeks later, she died.

I visited Wanda in the hospital. She wouldn't talk about her pain or her anger at these events. She seethed with it but kept it safely inside.

Anger and Repression, Anger and Illness

There are endless lists of names I could offer you and endless stories of women I know who have been "good, giving girls," who kept their anger inside, and who developed fatal tumours. I believe that there is a link between cancer and people who carry resentment. There may not be biological proof of this as yet, but there certainly is enough psychological evidence to connect repressed anger with cancer. (For additional information, please see the bibliography at the end of this book.)

To date there is there no known cure for cancer. Still, I've observed that psychopaths don't develop cancer: they're too busy acting out their issues. Come to think of it, it's the good folk who get tumours, the ones who rarely raise their voices, the ones who don't have the tantrums.

Of course, it is not only women who repress their anger or express it passively. John's story in Chapter Five is an example of a man who contained his anger and turned it inward. I have been addressing mostly women so far because it has been my experience that many men still retain the traditional belief that their role in life is to be strong and aggressive, and that their anger is permissible. They have "licence" to express their anger. It is exciting to see men changing their thinking and actions, becoming more aware of their own feelings and the feelings of others. It is encouraging to see men handle anger differently. The rising popularity of men's groups and the literature devoted to male issues attests to this change. (See bibliography for further reading.)

Many people, men as well as women, lead lives of quiet desperation. Like Lily, they don't express anger because they believe it is bad. They keep a lid on it until one day it blows off in a tornado of fury!

Does this sound like you?

Are you a person who feels that anger is bad? Do you stuff your feelings six feet under? Do you have secret resentments that stay secret? If so, you need to do something about it, and fast. Do this for your sake and for the sake of those around you.

You need to find a group you can share with, a support group. Join a self-help group. There are plenty around. Check your telephone directory. Or go to a local hospital and check their bulletin boards for support groups. If you know an alcoholic or have ever been involved with one, join Al-Anon. It's an excellent support group.

If you have difficulty acknowledging your own anger, the next chapter will start you on your journey. If you take your anger out on yourself, there is help at hand for you too. If you are someone who has trouble with tantrums, who uses a hit-and-run anger style, or who can't seem to control the criticisms and attacks that come out of your mouth, I have good news for you. It is possible to be free from this condition. If I can do it, so can you. So read on! Celebrate your daily victories with me. There is hope, I promise you.

Below is an exercise that will help anyone express anger

safely. I call it the three-second scream. It can be done anywhere, anytime, in front of anyone. It is a very simple and effective exercise that might just save your life! The next time you feel angry, regardless of where you are, use the three-second scream. People will think you are coughing or sneezing. You will really be discharging anger from your body, releasing yourself from any stress buildup, and freeing your throat so that you can then express yourself appropriately.

EXERCISE THREE
The Three-Second Scream

Take your right hand and cup it over your mouth. Take your left hand and place it firmly over your right hand. Hold both hands tight to your mouth and **SCREAM** at the top of your lungs. Try it now and see how it feels. Did you sound like a little mouse? Did you laugh at the strange sound that came out? Now that you know how to do this exercise make sure you practise it regularly.

I use it in board meetings. I use it when I am so frustrated I cannot bear one more phone call. I use it with my husband. I use it in front of clients. I use it in workshops and often in my car. (There I don't bother to muffle the sound with my hands. I just scream at top volume.) It won't cost you a penny, and it will save you from hurting yourself and alienating others.

Many of us suspect that we handle anger in a certain way, but that's not always the case. For example, I thought I handled my anger assertively. But after doing the following exercise I discovered I would run away after saying my piece. I also discovered that this was a combination of my mother's and father's styles of handling anger.

Here is an activity that will help you recognize your own anger style.

EXERCISE FOUR
Patterns of Anger in My Family and Me

Ask yourself:

a) How did my mother handle anger when I was young?

Write a description below.

b) How did my father handle anger when I was young?

Write a description below.

c) How do I handle anger now?

Be specific.

d) What did you learn from this exercise?

Write it below.

The intent here is not to blame anyone. I know your parents or guardians did the very best they could for you, just as their parents did the best they could for them. I know my parents did the best they could for me. Everyone makes mistakes. Each generation has its heritage. We are all victims of victims. That doesn't mean we should condone what has been done. Nor does it mean that we're entitled to dump on our parents, though we may do so for a time in therapy or in another safe setting, as we work it all through.

What *is* necessary is that we free ourselves. We need to take on the job of re-educating and healing ourselves. This is our job because there is no one who will ever care about us the way we can.

The good news is that we don't have to keep on paying the price for anyone's past mistakes. We can give ourselves a good education in living. We need to provide ourselves with tools that make the difference. We need to see where we build up our resentments and our anger defences **before** we can remove them. Remember, we can get free if we're willing to work at it.

I congratulate you on the work you have just completed. You have taken a major step in identifying your own anger style and in reclaiming your life. The next chapter is called "Instant Intervention," and it is intended to give you help and tools to deal with both repressed and raging anger styles. Remember, I'm with you each step of the way.

Chapter Four

Instant Intervention

To change one's life:
· Start immediately.
· Do it flamboyantly.
· No exceptions.

William James

Once you've identified your anger style you need to do something about it. You need **instant intervention**. Later, you can examine how your anger style dominates many aspects of your life but for now action is the key.

Let's start first with people who keep their anger hidden. You know who you are. You will still be good people when you allow your anger to surface. The difference is that you will deal directly with your feelings and be easier on yourself.

To begin, practise saying "No" instead of "Yes," even though it may feel wrong. Practise this "No" word. Instead of taking on extra work or picking up after someone else, say "No," and nothing else. That's all you have to do. No justifying or explaining. A simple "No." This might well be the most difficult word you have ever spoken. Say it anyway. You won't always be chained to saying "No," but for now it is imperative that you use it. Once you have done this for a while, it would be a good idea to get out a journal and write about your discoveries.

Now you are ready for more. Pick and choose from the following exercises or make up your own list.

EXERCISE FIVE
Instant Intervention Activities

1. Sing loudly when you're alone.

2. Take singing lessons: opera, jazz, or blues — anything where you have to let out your voice.

3. Register in a martial arts class.

4. Express your feelings, especially the angry ones with which you don't feel comfortable.

5. Do the exercises in this book, particularly the "three-second scream," the "pillow pound," "bat the bed," and "woodchopper." You will find them all in Chapter Ten under "Anger Tools."

6. Buy some crayons and paper. Choose the colour that represents anger to you and let go on paper.

By using some form of instant intervention, you begin to process your anger, so it doesn't stay trapped inside your body where it can hurt you. Don't think that because you don't feel anger you don't have it. I assure you this is not the case. We all do. If you have hidden your feelings from yourself, perhaps because it hasn't felt safe to express them, it doesn't mean you don't have them.

Tell your subconscious mind that it's okay to let your feelings out, that they won't kill or maim you or anyone else.

Do just one anger-acknowledging exercise today, and notice how good you feel. Keep track of this in your journal. Use the anger activities in this book as an ongoing anger workbook. Make sure you chart your progress. Remember, anger is a human emotion — one we all share.

If you can't feel your anger for the moment, that's fine. Just acknowledge that you have it somewhere. Maybe it's lodged in your elbow or your knee — the one that always hurts. **Think of your aches and pains. Do you have a pain in your shoulder? Do you feel this pain in particular moments or with certain people?** Are there people in your life that "give you a pain in the neck?"

Listen to your body

Make a physical inventory of your body. List any places that cause you discomfort or pain. Then ask each place what the pain is about. Write the answers in your notebook or journal.

Here are some examples others have recorded.

- My friend Mike had several months of severe aches and recurring flu after his mother moved, although he said he didn't miss her.

- When her marriage broke up, Alice suffered from backaches and a lot of pain near her heart.

- Gloria went back to work when her husband was laid off. She had to stand on her feet eight hours a day, and after a few weeks her arches dropped. She was angry that she was the only provider, and did not feel "supported" by her husband.

Pay attention to your body. Listen to it. Get help with your body needs. Tune into your inner voice. Ask yourself what your body needs, and believe what it has to say. You are your own best counsel, and it is important to follow your own good advice. Remember the wisdom of the ancient Chinese saying: " *To know and to not do, is not to know!*"

I'm not advocating that we spend our lives navel-gazing. Nor am I saying that it is wrong to look after people, to care for and to give unto others. We all need to give and receive. Our very future as individuals and as a society depends on this kind of exchange.

I am suggesting that we begin our charity at home with ourselves. We need to give to ourselves before we can give to anyone else. Otherwise we will walk around wounded, looking for someone to help or heal us, believing that if we do enough good deeds, if we are kind enough to others, eventually our turn will come, and we'll get back what we give out. If this is what we expect, then the reality that people often cannot or will not give back can easily lead us to anger.

The truest form of giving, and the one least likely to back-fire, is giving without expectation. We can only do that when we have enough self-nurturing to give freely, so that we don't need or expect anything back.

It is difficult to give to ourselves. That's why we don't do it. Many of us feel that we are not deserving, that we are not good enough. We find it much easier to give to others. So if you are a giver, start giving to yourself. Feed yourself pleasure. You can begin with any of the following suggestions.

EXERCISE SIX

- Take a walk.
- Go to a nearby park and use the swings.
- Call up a friend who makes you feel happy.
- Read that book you've been longing for.
- Play basketball or volleyball.
- Join an amateur theatre group.
- Take a bubble bath.
- Learn how to _____. (Fill in the blank with something you've always wanted to learn.)
- Take time for relaxation exercises.
- Do something just for you every single day and notice how good you begin to feel.

Here are some big ideas:

EXERCISE SEVEN

- Buy a painting.
- Throw out all the clothes you don't really love.
- Take riding or skiing lessons.
- If you're single, join a singles' interest group.
- Give yourself that compact disc player you've wanted.
- Go on a cruise.
- Join a health club.
- Go on a mountain-climbing expedition.
- Go on a spiritual retreat.
- Enrol in the best art classes going.
- Go for a weekend at the spa.
- Buy a new car.
- Learn how to scuba dive, and then go to the Caribbean to practise.

Do whatever it is you really want, and notice how good you feel inside. Notice how much more energy you have in other aspects of your life. Congratulate yourself on taking care of your needs. Give yourself a good pat on the back! Give yourself a hug. Keep on doing things for yourself. This is a lifelong prescription.

If you find yourself already debilitated with anger, if you are suffering from a disease, if you do have cancer, a heart condition, or arthritis, this next section is especially for you.

EXERCISE EIGHT

Think of your disease as your teacher. A dis-ease is a sense of not being at ease with our body. Sometimes it is a direct disconnection. To be at ease, we need bring our body and mind together. Start by speaking to your body. Ask it what it is that you need to learn and pay attention to the answers.

Our diseases and our distresses are our greatest teachers. For example, I used to have arthritis in my right shoulder and all the way down my arm. I found myself unable to play tennis or to lift heavy objects with that arm. It became increasingly painful. I ignored it for some years. Finally I found myself with a chronically painful condition. I had x-rays done. My doctor said "Yes, this is osteoarthritis." I felt like a victim. Then I got angry. I did not want to stay a victim so I got to work. I read a book called "How to cure your own arthritis." (See the bibliography.) For the first time in years I felt hopeful about my condition. I followed the instructions in the book, focusing on diet, exercise, and stress release. I went to a chiropractor and began to retrain my body. I made affirmations and used visualization. It took a lot of effort, but was well worth it. Today my shoulder feels fine and I can play tennis again.

If you have a disease, do whatever is necessary for you to heal yourself. This may include using both conventional and alternative therapies. You might begin with the following ideas.

- Use visualization and imagine yourself becoming healthy and balanced.

- Write out healing affirmations. For example, *I am healthy and energetic* or *Today I release tensions.*

- Follow a macro-biotic diet. (See the Bibliography for macro-biotic cookbooks.)

- Investigate vitamin therapy.

- Listen to self-healing tapes.

- Sing or speak your affirmations aloud.

- Watch funny videos.

- Practise yoga.

- Read self-help books.

- Use my anger tools.

Nurture yourself in whatever method works best for you. Become very pro-active and committed to your healing. Accept that you have this disease for a reason, and discover what that reason has to teach you. Remember, there is no blame implied here. The reason could be as simple as your needing to express yourself more. It may mean you need to work out some old memories. You may need to release some recent pain. It may mean you have to do less work for others.

Make sure you have people in your life with whom you can share your feelings, people to whom you can tell your truth. For example, there are many fine cancer and self-healing groups in existence. All you have to do is locate one. Start by making a telephone call, and follow through by joining the appropriate group.

Make sure you give yourself plenty of nurturance. Create a diet that includes vegetables, grains, fruit, and fibre on a daily basis. We are what we eat and we owe it to ourselves to eat foods that will sustain and revitalize us. There's an old adage that says, "If you want balance in your life, eat balancing foods." Think of colours that go together, that are in harmony, and create a palatable food medley of complementary colours. Or take yourself on a shopping trip without a grocery list. Instead, ask your body which food it NEEDS (not wants!), then buy your food accordingly.

Be careful of sugar. It plays havoc with the body, creating an immediate high and then a corresponding low. Pay attention to red meat if you wish to cut down on your anger. There have been studies linking aggression to the eating of red meat. Vegetables, grains, legumes, fish, poultry, and fresh fruit provide good balance for the body.

Here are some other nutritional tips:

- Use stainless steel, glass, or enamel cookware.

- Steam and undercook vegetables.

- Buy a water filter.

- Switch to herbal teas.

- Avoid white flour; use whole wheat flour. Buy multi-grain or whole wheat breads.

- Check food labels for additives, preservatives, and chemicals before you buy canned or dry goods.

- Be moderate with dairy foods, especially when you have colds. Dairy foods activate mucous production.

- When you eat Chinese food, ask to have it without MSG or sugar.

If you notice that you feel sluggish or depressed after eating, monitor your foods. One way you can do this is to eat only one vegetable at each meal for a week. For example, have a meal of rice or greens only to test your reaction. Keep a list of all the foods that enliven you and get rid of the ones that don't. Many of us are allergic to foods that we consume daily, and we wonder why we don't feel our best. If that applies to you, take responsibility for your nourishment. Remember, no one can take as good care of you as you can.

There are many books on food combining, balanced eating, and allergy-free living, some of which are listed in the bibliography. You can find them at any good bookstore. Think of your body as a car. Would you take your special car to any old roadside place and say "fill it up?" Would you give your car high octane gas? Your body is the temple of your soul. You are meant to take good care of it. Remember, this body has to last you for a lifetime, and what you feed it today will affect it in years to come.

Exercise according to your lifestyle

Speaking of your body, exercising it is vital. You don't have to force yourself into a regimented fitness program; just be conscious that your body needs to stretch, and your heart needs to circulate clean blood in order for your body to perform well.

Upon awakening, you can ease your body up by stretching into the day. Have you ever noticed how cats get up? They give themselves a long languorous stretch. We can certainly learn from cats, and either just stretch ourselves gently as we greet the day, or do some yoga or *tai chi* to prepare our bodies to carry us forth.

Another great exercise is walking. All you need is a good pair of shoes, and a little stretching before you take off. You can power walk, speed walk, or just walk-walk, but make sure you do it on a regular basis and for at least a half hour three times a week.

If walking is not for you, then swim, bike, or take up tennis. If these are not for you, try dance classes or low-impact aerobics. There is such a variety of exercise available. If you already know you won't stay on a program by yourself, find a walking buddy or a class to join. Make sure your exercise is balanced. You need both flexibility and blood circulation so create a routine that includes both stretching and pumping.

Remember, if you sit for much of the day, get up and stretch every so often. Your body needs it! Do neck rolls and shoulder lifts too!

One last thing. Get plenty of rest. We each need differing amounts of rest to feel good, and we each know how much sleep that is. For some folks five hours a night is plenty. Others need seven or eight hours. Give your body the rest it needs. This may mean taking a nap during the day. If you can't take a half-hour nap, you may be able to relax in your chair for 10 or 15 minutes at lunch and then get out for a walk.

Make the commitment to look after yourself so that you can receive maximum results from your life. Do the little things that make a difference. My mother used to tell me that the best sleep is the one with fresh air coming in the window, even in very cold weather. I don't know if this is true or not, but I always sleep better with the window open.

This chapter has been devoted to you taking care of you, because you deserve it. After all, you're the only you there will ever be! You are precious and remarkable. There will never be anyone else exactly like you. You are totally unique and you owe it to yourself to be good to yourself, to treat yourself well, to take care of your needs.

If you are doing this already, wonderful. Keep up the good work, and let me know what you are doing so I can pass it on to my readers. If you are just beginning, start with a step at a time. Pick up one new discipline and do it consistently. It makes no difference where you start, just pick one activity — either change your diet or get more rest or start to exercise — and commit yourself to action. You'll find the discipline you practise will automatically carry into other areas of your life. You will look and feel terrific!

Chapter Five

Thought Watching

*All that we are is the result
of what we have thought.*

Buddah

This chapter is about thoughts, specifically showing how our thought patterns influence our entire life. First, let me tell you Eric's story.

Eric was born on a boat coming to Canada from Denmark. His mother was a nurse. She had an affair with a married doctor and got pregnant. He gave her a substantial amount of money to quietly deal with her condition. She chose emigration to London, Ontario, thinking it would be like its namesake in England. This was in 1950.

London, Ontario, was a nice, small city. Eric's mother had her child, and looked after him for almost a year before she gave up. Small town life was not for her. She didn't want to be a single parent, so she gave Eric up for adoption and moved on.

The couple who adopted Eric couldn't have children. Eric's new dad really wanted a son, a namesake. They changed his name to John and bought him toys and clothes. The trouble was that Ellen, the new mother, didn't really want children, but she wanted to keep her husband. As it turned out, Ellen particularly didn't want boys, especially the active one she now had. The battle began.

Eric, now John, was a physical being, full of energy and activity. The bigger and stronger he grew, the more Ellen attacked and punished him. She had many unresolved anger issues brewing inside of her, and John seemed to trigger most of them. She would humiliate John in front of people. She called him a "dirty Danish bastard." She locked him in his room for hours at a time. She denied him privileges. When he talked back she took him out of sports, cutting off his main avenue of physical expression.

John's father tried to intervene, but he was a mild man who didn't like trouble. He found more work to do at the office and stayed there late into the nights. This gave Ellen total control of John.

By the time he was 15, John wanted to kill his mother. One day when she swore at him once too often, he picked up a knife. Fortunately, he realized that he was in trouble. Instead, he turned the knife on himself, slashed his arm, and ran away. He stole a car for transportation. He was picked up by the police. His mother lamented that John was evil, that he had tried to kill her, and that he needed to be locked up. John was sent to a "boys' farm" for a year.

When he was released, John started getting back at his mother and society. He stalked women, stole their money, and took their possessions. He was caught and sent to jail for another year. He became tougher and smarter. He resolved to stay out of trouble, and he kept his resolve.

By 20, John was a good-looking, well-built charmer who could sweet-talk almost any woman into giving him what he wanted. He wanted a lot. He got a job as a chauffeur, seduced the owner's wife, and then threatened her with blackmail. He was handsomely paid off.

John then bought his own taxi and did well as a driver. He was smart and he liked the freedom his business offered. He soon owned a fleet of cabs and was living the high life. He had lots of women, booze, and drugs. The only trouble was that he had a terrible temper, which became worse when he did drugs. He didn't hurt anyone except himself. He kept repeating the earlier pattern he had begun with his mother, the pattern of hurting himself, of turning the knife on his own body.

He now had scars zigzagging down his legs and arms. He had smashed fingers, bruised joints, and broken bones. He was also deeply lonely, for he could not stay in a relationship very long. There were plenty of women who genuinely loved him, but John just couldn't seem to hang in. Whenever they wanted "closeness" he would disappear.

By age 35, John was worth a lot of money. He was still a very good-looking man, intelligent, well-read, and elusive. He lived on his own and liked it that way. He had few friends. He found it hard to trust people. He had never spoken to his parents after he left London. He never discussed his anger or his pain with anyone. Although he owned a closet full of custom-tailored suits and state-of-the-art electronic equipment, John believed he was worthless, nothing but a dirty Danish bastard.

One day John got a sharp pain in his chest followed by nausea. He went to a doctor who sent him straight to the emergency department of a hospital. John had open heart surgery and barely made it. He had become so walled up with the pain of his past that his heart could no longer sustain his life. His arteries had virtually closed off his blood supply.

John felt he was unlovable. As an adult he had never allowed himself to get the love he needed. In his heart he believed all the things his mother had said to him. To recover, John needed to begin building his self-esteem. He learned to do so by using his anger as a pointer, as an indicator that there was something going on inside him that needed attention. He needed to release his anger in a safe way.

He learned to yell and pound pillows instead of hurting himself. He began to feel the pain he had repressed. He joined a "hug therapy" group that met three hours a week.

He worked with me on anger issues and thought-watching. I taught him to monitor his thoughts, to spend silent time listening to the messages he was giving himself, without acting upon them. We worked on cancelling these negative messages and implanting new positive thoughts.

His recovery was slow, but he made it. Today John is married and has two children. He is quick to praise these children, and slow to criticize them. John learned some important lessons from his own life. Today he shares his feelings. He knows that his life depends on it.

There are many men like John. Their histories are different, and some of them don't recover. They may have lofty positions in life. They may exert a lot of influence and power. But they don't love themselves any more than John did, and quite often they blow a gasket, suffering from heart attacks or high blood pressure. You hear about them dying at 38 or 45. These are men in the prime of their lives who have spent a lifetime denying their own feelings, never learning to truly care about themselves.

Release the "shoulds"

I believe that **we must love ourselves** first and foremost. If we do not, we will often become unhealthy, creating an exact physical disease to mirror our emotional disease. For example if we refuse to speak up for ourselves, we will get frequent throat infections. If we take on too much responsibility, if we live a life of "shoulds," then our shoulders will start to ache and sag. If we don't look after our own needs, our knees will let us know by hurting or eventually buckling, refusing to hold us up.

Our bodies are like thermostats. They let us know how we're doing and what areas we need to adjust. We need to listen to what our bodies are telling us, and then act on that information. We need to listen to our bodies and learn to love ourselves in a healthy manner. We also need to hear the thoughts we give ourselves, the internal messages, and begin to correct some of these messages.

For example, when you sleep in late, do you tell yourself that it was okay to sleep in, that you were tired and needed the rest? Are you grateful that you now have energy to do what you need to do? Or do you call yourself a fool for sleeping too late and not setting the alarm properly? How do you talk to yourself when you make mistakes? Do you give yourself loving feedback when you goof up or do you frequently criticize yourself?

Many of us treat ourselves like our worst enemies. We are constantly reprimanding ourselves. We think nasty, negative thoughts about ourselves. We think these thoughts and then believe them. When we do achieve something we can be proud of, we don't spend time taking in our accomplishment with a deep sense of satisfaction. We start another project immediately and push ourselves toward perfection.

Let's face it. Only a few of us got the love we needed as children. Most of us did not. We need to accept this fact. This does not mean that we can't ever get this love. We need to decide to give that love to ourselves. We need to begin by loving ourselves now, exactly as we are, human and fallible.

We need to give ourselves the love we didn't get

I believe the first step in self-love is to accept that we will never get what we needed from our parents because they simply didn't have it to give us. Like my mother used to say, "You can't get blood from a stone."

There is no point in focusing on how wrong our parents were. They loved us as best they could. There is no point in trying to get anyone to give what they can't. It's like smashing our heads against a brick wall! Nor is there any point in beating ourselves with the guilt stick of "I'm not good enough/I don't deserve love, etc." Sure, it hurts to realize that we can never change the past. It is hard to accept that fact. We need to grieve for the love we didn't get. We need to accept our losses, and we need to become willing to give ourselves what we need. This often means reparenting ourselves, treating ourselves with respect, understanding, and compassion. It is ongoing work that may continue for the rest of our lives.

We also need to be grateful and to love ourselves with that gratitude. We need to learn how to do it. Many of us don't have much of an idea of what loving ourselves means. We think it's something we can buy, like a candy bar, to soothe us. We think it's something we find in others or can get from them. We don't understand that love is discipline — it requires work and commitment to ourselves.

We need to learn the difference between "love of self" and "self-love." By self-love I mean an inflated ego around which everything must revolve. Self-love is making a big to-do about ourselves, puffing ourselves up like a giant balloon and then spreading our own hot air on everyone else. Self-love is a breeding ground for hostility and arrogance. Self-love is what Narcissus was practising when he was so busy adoring his own reflection in the water that he fell in.

We deserve love

Love of self, in contrast, is an appreciation of our dignity and value as human beings. Love of self is an expression of self-realization, and this expression brings forth the unique fruit that each one of us is meant to bear. Love of self is an honest acceptance of who and what we are. It's an awareness that **we don't have to do or be anything different** than we already are to deserve love. Love of self is unconditional or it's not love at all. When I talk about loving ourselves, I mean it in this context. Love of self is a continuous process of growth, with the amount of love available to us growing constantly.

Scott Peck, in his inspiring book, *The Road Less Travelled,* gives the best description of love that I have encountered. I urge you to read his book if you haven't already. In discussing love of self, Peck says:

63

We are incapable of loving another unless we love our-selves, just as we are incapable of teaching our chil-dren self-discipline unless we ourselves are self-disci-plined. It is actually impossible to forsake our own spiritual development in favour of someone else's. We cannot be a source of strength unless we nurture our own strength. Not only do [love of self] and love of others go hand in hand, ultimately they are indistin-guishable.

Your own anger, if you let it be your teacher, will guide you toward what you need to give to yourself. It will point you to the areas where you need to love yourself more. You won't know what those areas are if you don't watch your thoughts, so that is where you must begin. What we think is what we create. I have a poster on my kitchen wall with a thought jog from Yogi Amrit Desai, which reads:

You are the creator.
Whatever you think and believe,
that is what you create,
and that is what you become.

I read that poster every day. I need to be reminded that I am accountable for my own thoughts. As a woman thinketh, so she shall be. Think about it. Have you ever had the experi-ence of thinking about someone and then getting a letter from them or a phone call? Your thought was transferred to them or perhaps their thought was transferred to you. Thoughts are en-ergy and they vibrate with the meaning we give them. Thoughts are active. The dictionary defines a thought as "an act or the process of thinking." Science tells us that a thought is a short burst of energy that sends a signal to the brain. The brain doesn't care what the signal is about. It doesn't decipher what is good thinking and what is not. Like a computer, it simply acts on the material. If we send our brain lots of positive thoughts, it will act on this material. Our positive thoughts also act on our bodies. I've heard it said that if you want to know what a person is thinking, look at the state of their body. Does s/he carry a lot of pain or joy with him/her?

You can see why it is important to be aware of our thoughts, but how do we do this? There is a simple method described below.

The ancestor of every action is a thought.

Emerson

EXERCISE NINE
A Thinking Exercise

Find a quiet spot where you won't be disturbed. Shake out your body to release energy. Then sit comfortably and allow yourself to relax. Begin to take slow deep breaths, filling your abdomen and chest with oxygen, then slowly releasing it. When you feel relaxed, start to become aware of your thoughts. Simply notice your thoughts without judging them or holding onto them. See your thoughts as billboard messages that flash in front of you. Watch them pass by. Call them all "thinking." Do this process over and over again for at least 10 minutes. That's all there is to it.

Do this exercise regularly and you will begin to see which thoughts recur and what your thought patterns are. The important thing is to not judge your thoughts. Simply notice what you think, then let the thoughts go. We are not responsible for our thoughts. We *are* responsible for how long we hold onto them. This exercise is a method for becoming aware of our thoughts. Remember, we create our reality with the quality of our thinking.

Reprogram your thinking

Once you have been watching your thoughts for a while, and are able to spot the negative thoughts that you no longer wish to think, you can start reprogramming. Simply say, "Cancel, cancel," when you have a negative thought and replace it with a thought you prefer to have. Gradually, one thought at a time, you will build up a bank of empowering thoughts, and you will create a life that reflects this! For example if you should find yourself thinking "I'm too fat" (or too lazy, too old, etc.), or "I know I can never lose weight," or "I know I can never learn a new language," say, "Cancel, cancel," to that thought. Instead, think an empowering thought like, "I am now able to maintain my ideal weight," or, "I'm willing to learn a new language." The more you think this new empowering thought, the better you will feel about yourself. The better you feel, the more you will work at maintaining your ideal weight or accomplishing another challenging task.

It is truly awesome to realize how much power and control we can exert over our lives. We **are** the creators of our destiny. Our anger and our negativity are good tools for pointing out exactly what we need to focus on. So be grateful each time you catch yourself with a negative thought about you or anyone else. Accept it as a gift. Use the gift to work on yourself by changing your thinking and remember to love yourself in the process!

Chapter Six

Difficulties in Handling Conflict

*Everything that irritates us
about others can lead to an
understanding of ourselves.*

Carl Jung

Now that we have had time to understand ourselves, and observed our anger styles and our thought patterns, it is time to look at how we get into difficulty with others.

In this chapter we'll talk about some of the difficulties that most of us experience when we get into conflict with others. I will detail **The Big Five Booby Traps**, the ones where we often get stuck and stay stuck.

Booby Trap #1: PERCEPTUAL DISTORTION

The first and most pervasive difficulty we have is in what I call *perceptual distortion.*

If you have ever travelled, think back to a time when you went to a place you had never been, where people spoke a language you didn't understand. For a while you were probably in limbo, seeing people and things as if for the first time. Then you began associating people with those you knew back home, or you noticed signposts that were similar, and soon everything went "back to normal" again. You were no longer confused. You felt safe and in control. What you did was associate with part of your past and superimpose this onto your present environment. That's perceptual distortion in its simplest form.

Each one of us carries around our past conditioning. We go into new situations, and we see those situations through foggy glasses. It's almost as if we carry a big suitcase around with us. When we meet a new person we quickly take out costumes from our suitcase, drape these on the new person, and then say, "Aha," to ourselves, because we can now place them in recognizable outfits. We think we know who they are.

Perceptual distortion leads us to distort what we see. For example, take a moment to think about a time when you met someone you instantly disliked. You became angry when you thought about this person. You didn't know why. All you knew was that this person rubbed you the wrong way. You gave him/her a lot of room, and perhaps a nasty look. I call it "instant negative attraction."

Even though it feels as if it really is that person that you dislike, that there is something about how s/he is that annoys you, and it's her/his fault for being that way, **this is perceptual distortion**. What is really happening is that you are being triggered by your own past. Something about that person, maybe her hair style, or his glasses, or the way she walks or he talks, is triggering a negative association you have with someone in your past.

Become a detective

You need to disassociate with your projection. A good way to do this is to trace back the annoying gesture, mannerism, or physical feature to the original source. Then you can discover the connection, the "who" or "what" you're reacting to. Once you have done this, you can begin to see this person as s/he really is, free from your projection. Become a distortion detective so you can really see what is going on.

I used to get instantly angry when I encountered a woman with whom I worked. She was a large woman who had her hair permed in little sausage curls. I'd react to her requests with barely disguised hostility. Mostly I kept a safe distance from her. For years we had a distant and difficult relationship. When I learned about perceptual distortion, I realized that the woman in my second foster home, who used to hit me with an ironing cord and call me names, was also large and had little tight curls. I felt the anger churning inside me and realized I was projecting this anger onto the woman with whom I worked. My reaction was a clue that there was something I needed to look at in my past, an old resentment I had long held.

I told the woman I worked with what I had discovered. She said that she had always sensed that I didn't like her, so she had automatically disliked me. We were able to clear the air and gradually we became friends. I lost some of my shoulder pain in the process. There are times I still get triggered when encountering women who look like that woman in my foster home, but I now know what is going on and I can choose to let it go.

69

Another example:

You are at a gathering and suddenly, across the room, you see...**the one!** You know this is **the** person you've been waiting for, and so you find some excuse to go over and begin a conversation. Electricity is in the air.

You get together. The chemistry is fantastic. You decide to get involved and for a while everything is wonderful. One morning you wake up, look at that person lying there beside you, and you think, "I've made a terrible mistake. This is not **the one** at all!"

You are right. It is not and never was **the one**. What you did was fall in love with a piece of your past. Perhaps it was the curve of the cheek, the shape of the eyes, the way the person held his head, or the sound of her voice. You were triggered by some feature that reminded you of someone you loved when you were little. It could have been a parent, relative, or friend.

Seeing the entire picture

You superimposed that person on the person you met as an adult and fell in love with your own creation. It is thus a shock to suddenly realize that you are with a stranger. When you had that initial attraction and fell in love you "perceptually distorted." As we all have a history, and walk around with that history inside of us, none of us is free from perceptual distortion. We see "through a glass darkly." We see a bit of the picture, but not the entire picture. If you can remember this the next time you are triggered either positively or negatively, simply take the time to search inside yourself for the original source or inspiration for your feelings. Then you will begin to see more clearly and your perceptions will become less distorted.

By the way, if you have just discovered that the person you have a relationship with is not "the one," have a good laugh, and start to discover the wonderful qualities that person does have! This is where real love can begin.

Booby Trap #2: THINKING WE ARE "RIGHT"

Another difficulty that most of us have comes from thinking, fairly often, in various situations, that we are right. We love to be right. It gives us a sense of power, a sense of being in control.

Imagine you and I are having a conversation. You have just made a point and I respond by saying, "No, you don't get it. I know what is really going on and I know I'm right." How would you react? What would you feel, say, and do? If I insist on being right, what does that make you? How do you feel when you're made wrong? Not too good I bet. No one wants to be wrong. That's why we all have a big investment in being "**right!**"

This attitude maintains the illusion that we're in charge. At least in our own minds, we're superior. What does that do to our relationships with others? If we're superior, even in our thoughts, what are they?

Think back to when you were in elementary school. When the teacher asked for the answer in a math class, how many kids got it "right?" How about in history or spelling? How many "right" answers were there? What happened when someone got the right answer? What about the kids who got it "wrong," were they praised? Did they get the teacher's smile of approval?

We all want to be "right," because that way we feel important. We feel as if we matter. We need to feel important in our contacts with others. The problem is that we have it backwards. We need to matter to ourselves first. That takes some getting used to. We need to matter because we are ourselves, period, not because we are right or smart or know all the answers.

What is "right?"

Think about this for a moment. Is there a definite "right" way to say hello? Is there a "right" way to address someone when you meet socially? What is it? Now consider what happens in other countries. Do people greet each other the same way as we do here? Are they wrong or just different? In some countries and cultures it is impolite to look at a person straight in the eyes. Here we consider it impolite **not** to look straight in the eyes.

The way I see it, there is no right or wrong, just a different point of view. If you look at people from one perspective you see them a certain way. If you walk even a few feet away you see them differently. The same is true of ideas and opinions. If some ideas or opinions are not the same as ours, that does not mean that they are wrong, just that they are different.

We have been governed by laws, conditions, rituals, and beliefs that we often uphold and consider "right." We have an attachment to them. We buy in. We have a history. We have been socialized or conditioned to believe in these things. Often we're just plain lazy and take on other people's beliefs without even analysing them. That does not make them right or wrong, however.

Saying that we're "right," that our opinion or information is "right," immediately sets up an antagonistic situation. Remember this the next time you're tempted to take the bait. Remember how it feels to be made wrong. Instead, you can say, "That's an interesting point of view. I have a different perspective. Would you like to hear what it is?" The person to whom you are speaking may not be interested in hearing what you have to say, in which case it is not a good idea to force them to listen. You could also say, "The way I see it is ..." or "My belief is...." You could then listen to what the other person has to offer. Listening often encourages us to learn something new, and that's exciting. It keeps us growing.

Letting go of being "right"

I'm one of those people who has been very attached to being right. I still have to work diligently at letting go of my point of view. I notice this particularly in discussions with my husband. I want to prove a point or gather up evidence to make him agree with me. If he doesn't agree, then I often start to refute what he is saying and try to make him wrong. These days I notice that when I think I'm right, I also think "closed mind," because that is what I have. The way I see it, the most costly thing that I'll ever own is my own closed mind. I can't afford to keep it, so I keep investing in opening up my mind. The interest that I gain this way more than compensates for my old desire to be right. I see and learn more than I would have thought possible.

Booby Trap #3: THE VICTIM

"Poor me, I work harder than anyone else around here. I come in earlier. I do all the rotten jobs. Yet I don't get the raise or the praise. I just get ignored. It doesn't matter what I do, it's always the same."

Ever heard anyone talk like this before — maybe even you? This is the victim syndrome. Have you noticed that people who talk like this also have an investment in staying victims? For example if you try to talk victims out of their position, to show them other possibilities or even a solution, they usually don't want to hear you. They'll tell you that it won't work for them and may even tell you why. They don't want to do anything about their situation. Have you ever noticed this happening? If so, you've been interacting with victims. Don't bother trying to change them. Victims have a big investment in staying victims, so let them be.

Victims dig in their heels so that they won't have to change. They stay in their negative comfort zone and complain. This way they don't have to take risks. They don't have to confront themselves or others. They can stay the same.

There is absolutely no way to win with victims, so don't get upset. Let them talk for a little while. Then excuse yourself and go away. Perhaps they'll get the message. Most likely they'll find another rescuer with whom to play their game, but it won't be you! Victims can pull your energy down quickly, so don't stay around them too long.

If you live with one, get some help; you'll need it! Help for you! Al-Anon is a good support group, if you qualify. As is Co-Dependents Anonymous or Emotions Anonymous.

Listen to yourself

Now, what if **you** play the victim and can recognize it in these words? Well, good for you, because identifying actions is the first step in changing them. If you really wish to change your habits, the best place to start is with your own complaints.

Listen to yourself. Become aware when you start to complain and immediately substitute something for which you are grateful. This may seem awkward at first. It might even make for a disjointed conversation, but it does get easier with practice. Soon you'll develop a "cancel, cancel" method to reduce your complaining. Every time you start to think "poor me" or "woe is me," change into a different gear, and recognize the good things in your life. Begin with the basics. For example, you have a place to live. Right now, get out your pen and list 10 things you have to be grateful for. You can write them on the next page.

My Gratitude List

1.

2.

3.

4.

5.

6.

7.

8.

9.

10.

Remember these when you begin to complain, and shift into gratitude instead. Sure, there are days when we just want to draw the covers up over our eyes and go back to bed for the day — sometimes we need to do just that. There are also moments when it's great to vent our frustration and get it off our chest, as long as we don't verbally abuse someone else.

Notice your patterns. When you are complaining to someone, preface it by saying, "I just want to complain for a while." This way, the listener can choose whether to listen or not. If you want to discover the extent of your playing victim, spend more time on thought-watching and listen carefully to yourself. Listen to your tone of voice. Do you whine? Do you play "helpless?" Just notice what you do and begin to make corrections. Remember, the longest journey begins with the first step.

Booby Trap #4: A FAIR SOLUTION

You want a fair solution, but your boss, partner, or girlfriend does not. He or she seems blind to seeing this solution. This makes you really mad. This attitude (of yours) is a kissing cousin to the "I'm right, you're wrong" approach, because who's to say what's right or fair? Don't get caught up in "fair" terminology. Fair has to be fair for both, or it's not fair at all.

Booby Trap #5: UNDERHANDED METHODS OF OTHERS

How easy it is to spot what others do wrong. Have you ever noticed this? We sure can see when others are at fault, or when they're acting badly. We could certainly tell them how to do it better, if only they'd listen.

Why do you think it's so easy to see what others are doing, particularly when they do the "not nice" stuff, or they agitate us?

I have a theory.

I think we can look at life in two basic ways. I call these two ways "the blackboard" and "the mirror" approaches to life, because how we look determines what we see.

Basic Approach to Life # 1: THE BLACKBOARD

Using the blackboard approach to life, I can see what you're doing and it makes me mad. I criticize you, if only to myself. I judge you and condemn you in my own mind. I think, "How foolish you are," or, "What a slob you are." Or I get angry and tell you off. I get angry at you because of the way you slop your food or the way you speak to me. I get angry at your uncoordinated wardrobe or because you never arrive at work on time. I get angry because you won't stand up for yourself or you don't listen to my advice. We have hundreds of reasons for getting angry, all of them "triggered" by other people. That's the blackboard approach to life.

78

Here's an example: It's morning and I'm late for work. I can't find my car keys. The first thing that comes to my mind is my son's face. I know he has taken my keys. I just know it. Then I get angry at him because he has taken my keys. Now, I have not investigated this. It's just a feeling. But I'm angry and about to charge after him.

That's the blackboard approach to life.

Here's another example: There is a deadline to meet at work. Sam has given in all of his data ahead of time; Alex has not. Sam believes Alex is disorganized. He knows Alex is supposed to be the "creative" person, but he thinks that's hogwash. He thinks that Alex is simply disorganized and that he is extending the deadline. If only Alex was more organized, Sam's life would be smooth!

Living life with a blackboard approach means that any time we get angry we blame it on others. We believe it's their fault. For example, I get mad at you and blame you for whatever I don't like about you. I think it's your fault: you instigated my anger. I start to think of other things I don't like about you. I write this on my mental blackboard. I just write and write and keep on writing. Remember that a blackboard is not transparent or penetrable. It's always a one-way slate. I write out your wrongs because I can clearly see you and your faults. They glare at me. The more I mentally write, the more self-righteous I become.

If we live life with the blackboard approach we never have to see ourselves and we never have to change. Like the victim, we can keep on pointing the finger, listing other people's faults, concentrating on what shortcomings **they** have and what **they** do wrong. We don't need to do anything about ourselves. This can be a very comfortable way to live. That's why so many people do it.

Basic Approach to Life #2: THE MIRROR

Mirrors show reflections. They show us what we really look like when we look at them. They show us our good points and not-so-good ones too. When our anger is triggered by people — when we get angry at something someone does or does not do, when we get angry at something someone says or does not say, and when we use it as a mirror of what is inside ourselves — we can then see how we really are. We can get a composite picture of ourselves.

This is a difficult and sometimes painful process. We don't like to do it. We are shocked to discover that we have so many imperfections. Most of us have a desire for perfection. Often we believe that we really are quite perfect, and finding ourselves otherwise is quite disturbing. Perhaps we're afraid that if we don't like what we see, then others won't like us either, and so we avoid facing ourselves. We "hold up" our own image. We're afraid of rejection, so we refuse to look in the mirror.

For instance I get really mad at my chiropractor because he is frequently behind schedule, which means I have to wait long past the appointment time to see him. I sit in the waiting room anxious and impatient. In my mind I am never late; it is my chiropractor who has poor time management skills and is inconsiderate. As long as I stay mad at him, there is something inside me that I'm not seeing — something I'm protecting. I could ask myself, "When do I keep other people waiting?" or "Where am I inconsiderate?" and I bet if I asked myself these questions, I'd come up with some valuable information. I might see some of my own less-than-sterling qualities. This is valuable information because I would see that what irks me about him is also in me. Then I could deal with my chiropractor's lateness without any anger. I could let him know that I appreciate his skills but that I have difficulty with the waiting time. I could tell him that my time is valuable and that I cannot afford the hour wait. Then I could listen to what he has to say, knowing that I am handling my irritation in a positive and pro-active manner. He is now aware of my frustration. I'm not blaming him, I'm telling him how I feel and leaving the rest up to him. There is no emotional damage done. I've also had the benefit of looking at when I've been late or inconsiderate in my life. Perhaps I'll do something about it. That is the mirror approach.

When our anger is triggered by something someone else does, the mirror approach gives us an opportunity to look within and see what it reflects about us. We see our own Achilles heel.

This approach presupposes that we take responsibility for our actions. Using the mirror means stopping the blame game. It means speaking in "I" statements, for example "I feel," "I believe," or "I make myself angry," instead of "you make me feel" or "you make me angry." It means owning up and having the courage to look at ourselves as we really are, and then accepting it.

Accepting ourselves as we are is one of the most important ways we can love ourselves, because we can't love what we can't accept. Our acceptance of ourselves must be unconditional. Only then can we accept others as they are, warts and all, and not expect perfection.

The mirror approach takes away the illusions that can keep us separate from, and blaming of, others. Without the mirror we can't really see ourselves. We don't like to look at ourselves as we really are. We'll usually avoid it. We don't want the pain or the work.

Interestingly, the choice is always ours: blackboard or mirror. The rewards are also ours. We get to choose over and over again. Life is an endless banquet of choices.

These, then, are the **Five Big Booby Traps**:

1. Perceptual Distortion

2. Thinking We Are Right

3. The Victim

4. A Fair Solution

5. Seeing the Underhanded Methods of Others — Blackboard and Mirror

These are the typical traps most of us use to sabotage ourselves. I hope you've had an opportunity to recognize some of your own behaviour here. Thank yourself for looking and for seeing. Now it's time for a reward.

EXERCISE TEN

1. In the space below, write **four** things you love to do but have not been doing lately, e.g. go swimming, get a massage, go to the ball game, or listen to music.

2. Prioritize these according to your preferences.

3. Take out your daytimer or calendar. Write your number one choice in some time this week. Make it happen.

4. Write the remaining three choices in at some point during the next three months. You have now made room for the things you love to do in your life.

5. Repeat this process quarterly.

Chapter Seven

Releasing the Anger Ball

Do the thing, and you'll get
the energy to do the thing.

Leland Val Van de Wall

Picture this scenario. You are having a disagreement with your mate, and you are angry. The telephone rings. It's your best friend, wanting to take you to something special. At first you are a bit prickly, but gradually you relax and enjoy the conversation, laughing and chatting. You hang up feeling terrific. Then you turn around, see your mate, and wham! You're into the disagreement again, feeling angrier than ever. Did this ever happen to you?

Take another example.

You have a fight with someone you live with in the morning, go to work, spend a reasonably productive day, and come home feeling tired but content. You open the door and see "that" face. Suddenly you are angry again and begin fighting without skipping a beat. If this has happened, then you have been playing a game I call anger ball.

This is how we play anger ball.

We get upset and we project our hostility onto another person. Then we see them as sullen or angry. That's not all. We assume that their feelings toward us are equally hostile, so when we see them again, be it minutes or hours later, we act on this negative assumption and get our licks in first.

Or we withdraw first. We sulk and send out silent scorn, making sure they get our message.

Fight or flight, attack and withdraw, this defensive game goes on.

Picture yourself throwing an anger ball at someone. What do you think would happen? He'd probably throw it back to you, right? If so, you'd throw it back to him and you know what would happen next.

 Maybe he'd withdraw — physically, emotionally, or both. Then you might go after him. He'd withdraw some more, so you'd decide two can play this game. You'd retreat yourself, only you'd go even further away. When he came to get you, you wouldn't be "gotten."

It doesn't matter which style we assume. Fight or flight, they're both reactive, instinctive, and defensive styles. Usually our style acts as a catalyst. It intensifies the other person's hostility, and our original but false assumptions are reinforced. The war is on.

Here's an example.

Tracy works in human resources at a large insurance company. Last week Bob, the regional sales manager, discussed his training needs with Tracy. She gave him a list of the available seminars and workshops. When he responded by saying that the training didn't fulfil his needs, she patiently explained that because of budget restrictions no additional training would be offered through the company. Bob became angry. He told Tracy his sales staff needed immediate training in customer service so that they could bring in more customers and money, which would expand the budget. He spoke in a loud and aggressive manner. Then he told Tracy that he was going to speak to the president to make sure he got the additional training. Until this point Tracy was understanding, but as soon as Bob said he would go to the president, Tracy got angry.

She picked up the anger ball. She told Bob he could go where he liked as long as he didn't bother her again. Bob stormed out of her office. Tracy stewed for the rest of the day. When she went home that night she was sullen with her partner. She withdrew, curled up on the couch, and watched television. She slept badly. Two days later, Bob passed her  in the hall. He gave her a big hello and flashed a smile. Tracy shot him a dirty look, then averted her head. Who do you think was suffering? Tracy had picked up Bob's anger ball and she kept it close to her. Her body was sore, she was miserable, but she would not release the anger ball.

Here's another example. See if you can picture this scene.

EXERCISE ELEVEN

You're driving to work. It's a beautiful sunny day. You feel great. Suddenly a car swerves in front of you, almost causing a collision. You slam on the brakes and screech to a stop. Your heart is pounding, your hands are sweating, and you are mad! You get out of the car prepared to give the driver a piece of your mind and his car takes off.

Do you:

a) Yell?

b) Sulk?

c) Cry?

d) Spend a good part of the day talking about the insane drivers on the road?

e) Stay tensed up with stiffened shoulders that will later cause you pain?

f) Examine your options?

Which did you pick? If you chose 'a' and 'f' you are managing anger well and need to congratulate yourself. It is natural to get angry. It is vital to get the excess anger out of your body. Then you can have a good look at your choices. Did you know you always have choices? You can choose to praise yourself for handling an emergency, and handling it very well. You could give thanks for surviving a close call. You could be grateful that your car wasn't damaged. You could send prayers or kind thoughts to the other driver, because we both know that anyone who is driving like that is very stressed or in a state of frenzy. You could continue driving to work, empowered by the knowledge that you can handle difficult situations. You can choose to have a great day OR you can choose to stay angry and upset.

Choosing your reactions

If you choose to stay upset, then you can't blame the other driver for your emotional state. People **do** things. When someone does something and it affects you, it is your choice, your decision, to stay angry or to let it go. Come to think of it, the next time you're in the midst of any negative emotion — be it self-pity, guilt, feeling helpless, angry, hurt, envious, jealous, or depressed, ask yourself, "Is there anything happening right now that is causing me to feel this feeling?" If your answer is Yes, take a few deep breaths, do a few three-second anger screams, go for a walk, call a friend to vent your feelings, or write about it in your anger journal.

If the answer is No, chances are you're reacting to some unfinished business from the past — track it back so you can finish your healing.

The best way to let go of the anger ball is to realize you have choices. Take charge of the situation and choose *for* yourself. I've known people who held grudges against others for years, sometimes after they are long gone from this earth. Guess who suffers?

Similarly, when a fellow employee or client gets angry with us and attacks us verbally, most of us respond defensively, like

Tracy did. We defend ourselves and our company. We allow the situation to get to us. Sometimes we become involved in a shouting match or give someone "the cold shoulder." A much better idea would be to take a deep breath, stop for a moment, think, and then ask yourself, **"Is the client angry at me or the situation?"**

Usually it's the situation. You just happen to be there. So before you react, take time to recognize that the client is angry at the situation and not at you! Don't take it personally! Give yourself breathing room to respond so that you can have the calmness to do what is necessary.

Sometimes just listening is the best answer.

Often the best defence is none at all. Any time you catch yourself slipping into a defensive mode, take a few breaths instead. Breathe through your nose slowly and deeply. Breathe into your abdomen. Then take your breath up into your chest. Let the breath out of your nose or mouth. Repeat this three or four times. Your body will be the winner. Your emotions will not be frazzled. You will have the objectivity you need to concentrate on what really is at hand — the client's problem.

EXERCISE TWELVE
Dealing with a Client's Frustration

To help you do this you can:

• Take notes.

• Use paraphrasing techniques. Repeat what your client is saying using your own words, and check to see if you have the correct meaning.

- Ask questions.

- Be empathetic. Come from a feeling place.

Your client will end up feeling grateful and you will feel terrific!

Keep your anger journal with you and chronicle each time
you catch yourself throwing the anger ball, and note the ensu-
ing results. Notice how you feel. Write it down. When you are
critical and judgmental, catch yourself and make apologies. Own
up to your wrongdoings. Take responsibility for your own behaviour without being defensive.

Let go

Consider that the best defence is no defence. That's right, simply do away with defensiveness entirely. Instead, be vulner-
able. Have faith and let fear go. Adopt an open position. YOU
WILL NOT BE ANNIHILATED. You'll actually become
stronger. If you find this difficult, you might want to ask yourself how you perceive the universe. Is it a friendly place or not?
Depending upon your answer, you might want to work with
your belief system.

*Live your beliefs and you
can turn the world around.*

Henry Thoreau

When you do something you shouldn't, when you have hurt
someone inadvertently, admit it, apologize, ask for forgiveness,
and get on with life. If you are in the middle of berating someone, catch yourself, and ask yourself how you would feel if you

91

could love and accept this other person unconditionally. Then look at the person again. Notice what happens. Usually we see the other person, instead of seeing them through *our own perceptions.*

When we can let go of our defensive roles we are able to get to the heart of the matter and deal compassionately with whatever situation we find ourselves in.

We can practise mental *aikido*— which is to simply and non-aggressively move out of our own way, or away from someone else's line of fire.

In dropping the anger ball we maintain our sensibility and are able to move from game playing to problem solving, and to focus on solutions that are rewarding and empowering!

Chapter Eight

Stepping Out of Roles

When one door closes, another opens.

Helen Keller

One of the really sneaky things we do in life is to take on roles and then play these roles as if they were real. **We act.** We do this when we are angry or are being confronted. We adopt roles. Typically we play either the Parent, Child, or Adult role. We act out these roles as if they were our real parts.

For instance if I perceive that you have done something wrong, and I'm playing Parent, I'll probably get angry and want to punish you. I'll attack you or withdraw from you. If I'm playing Adult, I'll probably want to share my feelings about the situation with you, and ask how we can create a solution. If I play Child, I'll probably scream at you, sulk, want to hit you, and tell you to go away, saying, "I'm not your friend anymore."

Eric Berne founded this famous model of personality, comprised of three main ego states. Briefly, he stated that:

1. Our Adult state is our current thought state, our present moment.

2. Our Parent state, or our unexamined recorded state, is an exact copy of our own parents and the way they dealt with us.

3. Our Child state, our "felt" state, is the way we experienced life as a child.

Obviously, it would be great if we could all play the Adult role all the time, but then where would our wondrous child-like curious and playful selves be? Fortunately, we're human beings, growing and discovering, combining roles, making mistakes, being perfectly imperfect. We can't be any one thing all the time. What we need to do is become aware of the roles we are playing as close to the playing time as possible. This way we can identify the roles and share this knowledge with whomever we're with.

For example, some of us play the angry Child role over and over again. We may even notice that this role is not working for us very well, yet we are so caught up in the playing that it's as if we had no other options. We learn these roles and develop scripts early — perhaps in the sandbox. Here's a sampling of children's scripts.

ANDY: "Give me that shovel. If you don't give it to me I won't play with you."

BETTY: "I'm going to tell my mommy on you. Then you'll get into trouble."

CARL: "My dad is smarter than yours."

DONNA: "I don't care. I don't want to play with your truck. It looks stupid. I don't even like it."

We still use these scripts later on, except they sound more sophisticated. For example:

ANDY: "If you don't want to have sex with me, I know someone who does."

BETTY: "I don't want to talk to you. Call my lawyer."

CARL: "There are lots of people wanting your job. We're in a recession, remember?"

DONNA: "Listen, I didn't want to go out with you in the first place. It was my friend's idea, not mine."

Although the language sounds more mature, we're still playing the Child role, reacting with sulks, scorn, and sometimes savagery. What we need to do is understand this Child role, so that we can deal with it compassionately.

A. THE CHILD ROLE

Within each one of us there is a two-year-old who has tantrums. This child WANTS WHAT IT WANTS WHEN IT WANTS IT. Period. There is no delayed gratification possible.

EXERCISE THIRTEEN

Picture your inner two-year-old sitting high up on a purple cush-
ioned throne, smiling and playing. Now see what happens when
you say **No** to this child. What picture do you see? Draw or
describe it below.

This two-year-old is both charming and demanding. It
doesn't matter if you had good or poor parenting, the inner child
wants more, better, and constant attention. It's as if any time
your original child self didn't get its needs met it kept track and
out of these resentments it created an angry being of its own
making. This has become your tyrannical inner two-year-old.

No one ever got all his/her needs met. Each one of us has
stored rage. The Child acts out this foot-stomping fit of anger
for some of us, while in others it sulks and gets depressed, turning the anger inside, being in a perpetually resistant "I won't,
and you can't make me" mode of behaviour.

Making Friends with Your Inner Child

You need to befriend your inner Child so that you can let him/ her know you understand the rage. Let him/her know you know it's there, that it's perfectly normal, and that you appreciate the reasons, but that it's simply not appropriate to express behaviour this way. You want to keep the aliveness of the two-year-old because, after all, your Child is also curious, creative, and playful, and you want those qualities to remain with you. What your inner Child needs more than anything else is discipline, and you are the only one who can administer it. Remember, the best discipline is loving, gentle, and firm so that's the kind you need to give yourself. Being consistent is also important.

I have a very practical method to deal with my inner Child when she is having a tantrum. I use a script that goes like this: Silently I say, "Thank you for letting me know you're still there, but we're doing things differently now." I use this script when my Child threatens to sabotage me, when it wants to kick and scream and throw sand in someone's face. I use this when I need to *ask* for something instead of just demanding it. I use it when I just want to walk out that door and never return home. Often I do a three-second scream first, then I talk to my inner Child with this script. It works amazingly well for me. I feel as if I'm truly in charge. I'm not going to be tripped up by this little tyrant.

I also tell my inner Child that I care for her, and I assure her that we'll do some playing soon, because my Child self has a right to have fun. I have asked her what she likes to play with, and have gone and bought us some paper dolls, some finger paint, some beautiful gold and silver crayons, and some Nerf balls. I keep my promises to my inner Child; I value her immensely.

97

This method works well for me. Feel free to invent and vary the dialogue for your own use, and remember to include a loving comment at the end. When it comes time to play with your inner child, just ask the little person what s/he wants and you'll have a great time! I guess that's why grandmothers and grandfathers are so good with little kids, they get another legitimate chance to play. We don't have to become a grandparent to play. We can do it right now.

If you would like to access your inner Child and don't know where to start, try this exercise.

EXERCISE FOURTEEN

Ask your inner Child to write you a letter. Give this Child permission. Assure her/him that you will understand what s/he says. Pick up a pencil and write with your non-dominant hand. Give yourself both time and patience.

Letter from my inner Child

98

It is important that you communicate with your inner Child in a positive manner. Your sense of well-being, your daily experiences, and the joy you create will increase when you spend constructive time with this inner Child.

B. THE PARENT ROLE

We use this when we have a vested interest in being right. All of us play the Parent role from time to time (and I'm not talking about parenting our own children here!).

My eldest daughter likes to play Parent with me. I played Parent with my mother, and I often attempt to use it on my husband.

For instance you may find yourself correcting someone, being critical, or telling her what she *should* do without her asking your advice. You may notice that you tend to criticize or berate your partner, instead of just listening. You might discover that you nag instead of asking why s/he didn't complete a job.

We play the Parent role just as we play the Child. In fact, we often hookup with a person who is acting out the Child role, so we adopt the Parent role instantly. An excellent analogy for how the various roles work is in a marriage or committed relationship.

There are usually six people operating within the two partners of a relationship. Both people have Child, Parent, and Adult selves with which to interact. Often one partner will play the Parent role more visibly. Sometimes it's the wife (or the partner who is playing the "wife" role) who believes she is the guardian of what is appropriate or right in any given situation. For example, she will correct her partner's table manners. She will tell him to take off the tie he is wearing, explaining that it doesn't go with the shirt. The wife usually plays this role because that's what she saw her own mother do. Many men play Parent as well. They take on the role of disciplinarian, or final arbiter on financial matters. Often they are in charge of planning trips or have the last word on those big decisions.

There is always someone who plays Parent at work, and it is not necessarily the boss. If you can think of someone who invariably has the "right" answer, who, when you come up with a plan or an idea usually has a better one, this may well be someone who is playing Parent.

If you notice yourself playing the Parent role a tad too frequently, and you want to stop doing it, great. I have good news for you. There is a solution, and it's simple. All you need to do is keep your mouth shut. Say nothing. When someone is telling you about something they're doing and you think it's a lousy idea, say nothing. Even if you want to scream, just nod your head and smile encouragingly.

Who put me in charge?

If you have a friend/mate who wants to play music and you think s/he is tone-deaf, say nothing. Weigh the consequences first. Is it more important that your friend express himself/herself or that you put a damper on this expression? Sure, you may have to buy earplugs, but so what!

A good question to ask yourself whenever you want to tell someone what they *should* be doing is, "Who put **me** in charge of their life?"

Similarly, if someone has an idea for a project that is different than yours — one that could possibly work — say nothing

101

and let that person's idea reverberate for a while. Maybe it's a good idea, maybe it's not, but it's that person's idea and it's up to him/her to test it out.

The Wright brothers flew right through the smokescreen of Impossibility.

Charles F. Kettering

Recently, I was leading a conflict session for a group of managers. They supervised the lead hands who make plastic containers from moulds. We were discussing the importance of letting go of the Parent role and saying nothing, and they brought up the following anecdote.

One of the lead hands came up with the idea that two moulds could be combined, so that a third and more innovative mould could be produced. An engineer calculated the figures and said it could not be done.

The manager knew a similar idea had failed before. He told the lead hand that it was a good idea, but not feasible. He had data and figures as backup. The lead hand was so enthusiastic and so convinced it would work that the manager decided to be quiet and give it a try. Guess what? The impossible happened. A new creation was born. The company was able to sell this product to new and old clients alike, both productivity and profitability increased, and morale was very high.

Now I realize every situation is different, but how will we know what could happen if we veto different approaches? What would have happened if Alexander Graham Bell had listened to the naysayers? Or Sojourner Truth? Or Roger Bannister? Or Golda Meir? It is vital for us to let go of playing the Parent role if we want to encourage creativity.

Recognizing when we are playing the Parent is difficult, particularly when we've been doing it for a long time. If you like to have the last word, if you have difficulty just listening without giving advice, or if you want to play "one-up-manship," they are clear signs that you've been playing the Parent role.

One of the best ways of recognizing the Parent role is to use the mirror approach to life. Remember, mirrors reflect us so if you get upset when someone is telling *you* what to do, it's likely that *you* play the Parent yourself!

Of course there are good things about the Parent role, and the best is being able to parent ourselves. Then we get to become adults who know ourselves and can act from this vantage point. We are able to laugh at our regressions, and not take ourselves so seriously! I call this role "the balanced adult" because it is indeed a balancing act.

C. THE BALANCED ADULT

This is a person who can recognize roles s/he may be playing and 'fess up to them The balanced adult is able to play Parent when a quick decision is called for, and can use the Child's curiosity and openness to continuous advantage in life.

Being a balanced adult is both fun and challenging. It is never boring. Like any balancing act, this one takes practice, for we all have feelings and habits. We have attitudes and actions that we need to change.

Change *is* difficult. Many of us resist change even though we pretend we don't. The very thought of change can trigger our resistance. For example, I know people who resist each season, even though they live in a country of four distinct seasons. My friend Ellen needs a haircut, yet she resists going to a new stylist even though she complains that her present stylist never does what she wants. She knows she needs a change, yet she resists it.

We need to know that we resist change. We need to give ourselves this understanding. We might even give ourselves permission to resist for a while. We also need to move on from this resistance or we'll stagnate. When we spend our lives resisting we ultimately end up living life like a rock in a hard place.

Changing behaviour requires courage

The word courage comes from the French word 'coeur,' meaning heart. We need to take heart. Even though we might be afraid, we take heart and make the change anyway.

One of the most astonishing things about courage is that we can't have it without having fear. I once thought that courage meant I was not supposed to feel fear, that somehow courage was a "pure" state. What nonsense that was! Courage means to take heart in the very midst of fear. We need courage to deal with our own resistance to change.

So take heart. If the playing of any of these roles — be it Child or Parent — applies to you, I'm delighted because now you know what you can do to change. You can drop the role. You can alter the behaviour. The truth will set you free as long as you're prepared to see it.

Remember to be gentle with yourself in the process.

You **will** make mis-takes. (A mis-take is simply a chance to take it again.) So pick yourself up, dust yourself off, and keep on going. I promise you, it does get easier, and the results are well worth it!

Next is an activity you can use to identify and change a role you might be playing.

EXERCISE FIFTEEN

1) Think of an area in your life where you are experiencing a conflict. It could be at work or in a relationship. It could be over politics or a social situation. Pick an area that you find troublesome. Then write it below.

2) Decide which of your roles is creating this conflict. Close your eyes and imagine what this role looks like. Are you young or old? How do you speak? What expressions do you use? How do you dress?

3) Ask this part of you if it would be willing to experiment with doing things differently. If you get permission, then ask this part to take on a different role, one that would contribute to your growth and higher good. Write what this new scenario would look like.

4) Close your eyes and look again at this part of yourself. Do you look any different? Are you any younger or older? Do you dress differently? Thank this part of yourself for being so helpful and willing to change for your overall good.

Chapter Nine

Hot Flashes and Anger Triggers

*Your vision will become clear
only when you can look
into your own heart.
Who looks outside, dreams;
who looks inside, awakens.*

Carl Jung

For as long as we live, our anger will be triggered by people, places, and things. No matter how much we know and understand ourselves and others, despite all our good intentions, our readings, and our use of the anger tools, our anger will still be triggered.

I think this is good news. First of all, when our anger is triggered, we know we're human and alive. Second, we get to see what we need to work on next. Third, we receive a gift of understanding, which can teach us more about ourselves and others, if we accept it.

So let's take a look at some of these triggers or hot flashes. What causes the ire to burn within us?

EXERCISE SIXTEEN

Get out a piece of paper and specifically look at what triggers your anger. What is it that people do that makes you mad?

- Arrogant people?
- Someone who criticizes you?
- Someone who undermines you?
- "Know it alls?"
- People who arrive late and leave early?
- Dishonest people?
- Intolerance?
- Inconsiderate people?
- Co-workers who state, "It's not my job," when you ask them to do something?
- Co-workers who don't do a proper job, so that you have to redo it for them?

Take some time and write out which character traits drive you bananas and remember the truth WILL set you free.

Now look at some other habits people have. For example:

- Drivers who race by you, exceeding the speed limit.

- People who drive in the passing lane at an excruciatingly slow pace.

- How about politicians? Do any of them have habits that annoy you?

What are the things your mate does that send you screeching (at least on the inside)? Toothpaste cap left off? Clothes thrown on the floor? That annoying throat clearing? List them below.

Anger Triggers

Once you have a sizable list completed, say at least 10 triggers, go through the list and ask yourself this question about each one: "Have I ever done this?"

For example if being criticized is something that makes you mad, ask yourself, "Have I ever criticized anyone?"

Or if irresponsible people get you going, then ask yourself, "Have I ever been irresponsible?"

Do this with each characteristic that triggers you.

Write a "Yes" (I have done this) or a "No" beside your own list.

For example:

Triggers	Yes	No
Irresponsibility		
Dishonesty		
Lateness		

At the end of your list, total up the Yeses. (I want you to know that I have many Yeses on my list, so don't feel upset if you do too.)

Remember, we get upset at the habits *we ourselves have* and don't want to acknowledge; otherwise, they wouldn't bother us. So this list is really about discovering yourself and the areas you need to work on. Triggers are really liberation points, if we choose to look at them this way.

Once you've gone through your list, circle the one that gets you the most angry. Once you've done that, go back in time and see who did this very thing to you. For example, who criticized you when you were little? How did you feel then? What is it you wanted to do to them? Write your discovery below.

Forgiveness is for you

When you have finished, forgive them. To forgive means to give as before, so forgive what they did or said; they were doing the best they could at the time and they were human just like you. To forgive means to restore the person in your own mind and heart, so you can see them without holding any resentment toward them. If you can't forgive, ask for the willingness to do so. If you can't pray, ask God or your higher self or the universe to give you the willingness to forgive. Ask for help with forgiveness so that you can be whole. Please understand that forgiveness is really about you, about healing your own life. Know that any feeling of anger you harbour for another being hurts *you* and keeps *you* in that other's power. So make the choice to free yourself by this act of forgiveness.

You could also write a letter of forgiveness to the person with whom you're angry. You don't have to send this letter, just write it. Remember, forgiveness is *for* you, so you can give back to yourself the part of you that has been holding a grudge.

Are you with me? Great. We're ready to go on.

Now here comes the exciting part. I want you to understand this, because it is fundamental to your self-acceptance and your own growth.

NO ONE CAN MAKE YOU ANGRY.

YOU MAKE YOURSELF ANGRY.

YOU CHOOSE TO GET ANGRY.

Read these statements over and over again.

No extenuating circumstances, nothing anyone says or does can make you angry. This is a fact. Yes, I know you have examples of times people made you angry. So did I. The very notion that no one else makes you angry is reason enough to slam this book shut! But stay with it, remember, keep an open mind! You want the truth, I know you do, and the truth is simple. No one can make you angry. You make yourself angry. You do this because it's a habit you've created to keep you safe. It's a protection so that you don't have to really see yourself and perhaps feel the pain this insight may bring. Remember you have choices. You can choose to be courageous and use the mirror approach. No one likes to look at their own imperfections. We would rather get angry at others. That way we feel safe and we don't have to deal with our imperfections. You are no different. When you believe that someone else makes you angry, you don't have to take responsibility for your reactions. There is no risk of rejection. You maintain the illusion that you really are almost perfect. This is called denial.

We all practise denial. Very few people ever really want to know the truth when it comes to themselves. We prefer to use the blackboard approach. That's why we need other people, and why it is so important to understand what triggers our anger.

We make ourselves angry

We also **make** ourselves upset or afraid. Other people **do** things, but that is simply what they do, our reaction is entirely up to us. If someone directs their anger toward us, the tendency is to get hooked. However, choosing consciously means we can do something else. We can detach. We can feel compassion for them.

It's when we put ourselves in the picture that we get into trouble. The choice is always ours. In his play *Othello,* Shakespeare said, *"Thou has not half the power to do me harm, as I have to be hurt."*

Once again the choice is ours.

For example if I said to you, "Hey, you have a purple nose," would you get upset? Probably not because you know it is not true. However, what would happen if I said, "You are a selfish and inconsiderate person." How would you feel then? A little uncomfortable perhaps? From time to time each one of us suffers from a lack of self-esteem. If I accused you of being selfish and inconsiderate at one of those times, you would likely react with anger. This is still your choice. Because our self-esteem is not up to scratch, when someone says something to us that *might* contain a grain of truth, we take it as a criticism and get upset. We forget that we have a choice; we could simply listen and act as if they were saying we had a purple nose. We don't have to take it personally.

The choice is ours

We need to decide who has the power? Who's in charge of us? Do we keep our power or give it away? Do we give our power away to **them** by reacting? *Do we become victims* when they push our triggers? Do we let self-pity tangle us up? Can we detach? Are we willing to see that it is merely a person who is trying to goad us, or trying to make themselves feel better by acting superior?

It doesn't matter what their motive is, we have enough to do in looking after ourselves, checking out our own motives. It's a full-time job, one that requires information, strategy, and tools. We need to concentrate this energy where it belongs, on ourselves, being mindful of our own reactions.

114

When we can do that, we have a good chance at saving any situation that could otherwise disintegrate into a retaliation match. Each little battle that we win *with ourselves* makes the next one easier.

Hot flashes

Hot flashes are great information givers. Usually we get a hot flash about some area in which we feel shame. This is a good indication that we still have internal work to do. If we get a hot flash and do nothing about it, chances are a resentment will start building. We need to feel the flash, be conscious of what it is telling us, and take the next step. If we are being humiliated, do we say something? Do we say, "I feel hurt when you make fun of me," and then let the other person have the opportunity to look at their behaviour?

Do we use the hot flash as a guide?

This refers to both the regular anger flash and the hot flashes that come with menopause. I can't speak for the male menopause, but I can for the female variety, as I am now in the midst of it. Although I have not had many physical hot flashes, I do get an increase of anger flare-ups these days, and have to remember that my hormones are doing their own dance. I notice that I am more irritable, have less patience, am edgy, jittery, and prone to outbursts. I keep these facts in mind when I get instantly flushed. It helps me to remember that I can drink calming teas or that I can brew some mistletoe to regulate my body temperature. This also helps me to apply the necessary anger tools as I need them. I use the hot flash as an awareness guide. Most of the time this awareness works well for me.

Creating serenity

Whether we react with hot flashes or anger triggers, there is a special prayer that can help. For some of us the word "prayer" is a trigger. It evokes memories of organized religion or perhaps memories of being forced to repeat senseless words. If that's the case, consider a new definition of prayer. It is simply a useful tool.

This prayer is called The Serenity Prayer and it goes like this:

**GOD, GRANT ME THE SERENITY
TO ACCEPT THE THINGS I CAN NOT CHANGE,
COURAGE TO CHANGE THE THINGS I CAN,
AND WISDOM TO KNOW THE DIFFERENCE.**

I say this prayer many times a day. My interpretation of it is as follows:

Unless I ask for help, I won't get any, so **God**, please help me. (If you don't like the word "God," remember "God" can stand for Good Orderly Direction.)

Grant me the serenity

I can't do anything effectively when I'm disturbed. My thinking goes out of whack, so first I need to be centred. I need to become serene.

To accept the things I cannot change

I cannot change the weather, traffic, my neighbour, my spouse, or the past. There's a whole lot more I cannot change. I used to try to change my husband — what a waste of energy! I made myself furious in the process. Being a slow learner, I also used to try to change my son, my daughters, my friends, associates, clients, etc. Today I actually accept that I cannot change anyone except myself. What a relief for everyone!

Courage to change the things I can

Primarily that means me. I can change my attitude. I can change my behaviour. Whenever I wake up feeling grumpy, I can practise energetic breathing or make a list of all the things for which I have to be grateful. I can call a friend and vent a little steam. I have choices. I don't need to stay upset.

I can also change my beliefs. I can look at what I really do believe and what I've simply absorbed from other people. I can discard those beliefs that no longer work for me.

I can change my habits. It will take me time, but I can change them. I've already stopped drinking, smoking, taking pills, lying, and stealing. I now meditate, exercise, tell the truth, circulate money, and trust people. I have many choices and new habits.

Doing the inner work

Working on me takes time and energy. I believe that if each one of us did our own inner work, we would not need the police to protect us. We would be a self-governing community of people who acted in full consciousness. I'm convinced that my job on earth is to make **me** the best **me** I can be. This is a full-time job I can assure you!

Once I affirm that my work in life is to work on me, I have a lot to do!

- I can use courage to change the things I can in my world.

- I can speak up when I see wrong.

- I can become part of the solution.

- I can stand up for myself.

- I can join committees and associations.

- I can ask for what I need.

- I can be on a board of directors and make a significant contribution to my community and to my world.

- I don't have to grind axes. I am a valuable asset because I can be objective.

Wisdom to know the difference

This means check in time. I ask myself several questions, for instance:

- Am I putting off doing something about me by transferring blame to you?

- Am I falling into my old ways again?

- Do I really believe I can still change other people?

- Am I doing the work I need to do on me?

- What is important for me to act on?

- What do I need to let go of?

This prayer is a gem because it is so concise and it invites personal action. To me it sums up the reality of being responsible. If you are not already using this prayer, why not give it a chance?

Anger can be a coverup

When you catch yourself getting angry and saying, "I get so mad when you interrupt me," start saying, "I make myself mad." This may sound strange at first, and you might resist doing it. That's okay, but be aware that it really does remind you to put responsibility where it belongs.

Instead of saying, "Why did s/he do this to me?" ask, "Why did s/he do this?" Take yourself right out of the picture.

Understand that a lot of the anger we feel is a ruse, a cover-up. We can release our anger, get it right out of our bodies, then look inside at what's really going on.

For example yesterday I got angry when one of my associates mistakenly kicked the computer plug out of the wall socket, and my program crashed. All my writing was lost. I was furious. I yelled. I wanted to scream *at* her, make her responsible, punish her (my "Parent" was outraged). I wanted to really let her have it (my "Child" wanted to get in on the act too). I felt such blame, yet in the same moment I knew better, so l quickly yelled my anger out. (I did two hand-over-mouth three-second screams.)

Then I added words. I said I was angry, and then I said I made myself angry. I'd spent the entire morning writing this material, which comes from my head, and there was no other source or copy available. I didn't have any of it jotted down. It was gone. How would I replace it?

I mourned the loss. Then I admitted feeling like a victim, and, of course, realized I was a victim of my own negligence. It was me who had not saved my material. I hadn't even known there was a save command on my computer.

My own ignorance had hurt me

I remembered a quote from Isaac Meier. "You have done wrong? Then balance it by doing right." I got to work. First I re-arranged the plug so that the same thing could not happen again. Then I began rewriting what I could remember, calming myself in the process, discovering that my thoughts were more orderly this time, as if I had already edited the material.

I acknowledged that my mind was working well, and felt grateful. Then I learned how to save my material and zealously pressed the save command all afternoon. Later I went out and bought myself some discs so I had a backup system.

Do you think I learned a lot from this situation?

The best parts were that I didn't alienate my associate, give myself an anger hangover, or smash my computer. I handled it. Did I feel good? You bet I did. I celebrated my victory all afternoon as I wrote the hours away. Do I respond this way all the time? What do you think? It has been immeasurably helpful for me to use responsible language. To say, "I make myself angry," when I start to feel the flame rising, or, "I scare myself," when I'm in the passing lane and need to get in front of that big transport truck. When I do this I automatically empower myself.

I also get to understand my habitual behaviour, and can begin to change it. Now I understand that my anger is often a cover-up for sadness, and that "shoot first, ask questions later" is my automatic response. Understanding has given me options. I can choose to do something different. You know the saying, "If we always do what we've always done, then we'll always get what we've always gotten." Bad English, good sense.

When I am triggered, I usually go red or numb. My ego is in charge. I am in big danger. Instead of attacking or blaming, I can choose to get out the feeling and then be quiet. I can begin to think.

Staying angry can be easier than changing behaviour

When I first got angry about the computer incident, I didn't experience the anguish of self-confrontation. I felt I had been "done to" and I reacted instantly by yelling. That was fine for that moment. The truth is I have never had computer training, and because I don't understand the manual, I avoid it. The resistant part of me was in operation. As long as I stayed angry, I didn't have to face myself and face that I needed to make some changes.

It is hard to fight an enemy who has outposts in your head.

Sally Kempton

I don't like change any more than anyone else. I have old behaviour patterns that are hard to break. For example, there are occasions when I *feel* rejected by my husband and l verbally attack him, or close off and withdraw. I know this is an old habit, and sometimes I fall victim to my habitual responses.

I still use anger to avoid emotional pain. Last week my 20-year-old son called to tell me he'd had a bike accident and lost his two front teeth. It was a late night accident, and I suspected he'd been drinking. He is working as an actor this summer, so this is a very tangible loss. Immediately, I became angry. I inappropriately yelled at him. My anger staved off the pain of feeling his pain. My anger put me on the offensive. It enabled me to react in my old pattern, which goes like this. "If I get angry at something he's done, then he doesn't have to be upset at himself. He can get angry back at me, and not have to look at his own actions. If I get angry at him I don't have to feel guilty about not being a good mother, and not preparing my son to face life better."

I know this and I have a lifetime habit of keeping pain away — both mine and his. Using anger also kept me from feeling the fear that my son was into self-destructive behaviour. So I got off the telephone, said the Serenity Prayer *until I was serene*, called him back, apologized for my reaction, said I was sorry he was hurt, and asked him what he was going to do to take care of himself.

Sometimes I am able to catch my anger and nip it in the bud; other times I cannot. In the long run I'm getting better. I don't expect miracles or overnight changes. I accept my foibles and do my best to correct the damage.

There will always be triggers

Triggers? Hot flashes? Yes indeed, there will always be triggers. Even when you know that you're reacting to someone and the original source is in the past, even then there are times you'll just want to act your anger out, and there will be times when you do. When this happens, forgive yourself, and do the repair work. Yes, it's better to beat a pillow than to harm a human being, you or anyone else. And yes, we are human. We each have to live with the remorse our anger generates until we are well versed in doing things differently.

I figure it is all "work-in-progress." This involves identifying our triggers, understanding what gets us going, taking immediate responsibility for our behaviour, and then using some of the anger tools. It is well worth the effort!

If we're willing to make changes, we can keep our self-respect. We discover gifts in every situation and we enhance our knowledge. We learn how to use anger as a catalyst for growth. We celebrate our triggers and hot flashes because we know they are opportunities for us to work on ourselves. We need to be vigilant and committed, and at the same time willing to give ourselves room for error. We need to accept that we will make mistakes. By owning up to these mistakes, by forgiving ourselves and asking others to forgive us, we build up our dignity and enlarge our humanity.

EXERCISE SEVENTEEN

Take a situation — any situation — where you recently got triggered. Write it below.

Then ask yourself, "At what point did I choose to get angry?" Write about this too.

This way you begin to see where your triggers begin and you can use some of the anger tools to protect yourself.

Chapter Ten

Anger Tools

There is no security on this earth,
there is only opportunity.

General MacArthur

HERE THEY ARE AT LAST!

This chapter contains a wealth of anger tools; some are effective on a short-term basis and some on a long-term. They are a carefully selected assortment of tools with which I have had success.

These tools are not arranged in any particular order, so what I suggest is that you try the ones that appeal to you and note the results. Then you can add or delete from this list, creating your own personal tool kit.

1) THREE-SECOND SCREAM

Take your right hand and cover your mouth. Take your left hand and place it firmly on top of your right hand. Count to three, inhale, and then scream at the top of your lungs. Notice what happens. You can barely hear yourself, right? So do it again. How does your throat feel? A little sore? That's okay; it will pass. Did you laugh? Did you feel freer?

You can use this scream anywhere — at your desk or in front of company. Just bend your head when you do it and they'll think you're coughing. It gets rid of anger instantly, clears your throat, and takes any buildup away. If you are the type who wants to say deadly things and have come to realize how damaging this behaviour is, then the three-second scream will come in handy. If you're a "shoot first" person, try "scream first" instead. It cuts down on casualties.

Use the three-second scream whenever you feel anger rising in your body. Even if it's just at the ankle level, you can get rid of the angry energy before it overtakes you. I will often excuse myself from a meeting, go to the washroom, and have a good scream. If I have to excuse myself several times in the course of a meeting, I'll do it. People may think I have a weak bladder. That's okay; it's a lot better than seeing me as an assassin. I use the three-second scream in line-ups and other times when I'm feeling impatient. No one has ever been startled. Most people don't even notice what I'm doing. I use it during telephone calls (I put the receiver down first.) I use it in my car. When I'm driving alone, I don't cover my mouth. I just yell.

Even if you feel you don't have anger, start using the three-second scream. It will help clear any unconscious, stored-up anger out of your body.

2) WOODCHOPPER

Woodchopping is what many people used to do before they moved to the city. It's a "breathe, raise the arms, and let go" process, and it's a great way of getting rid of body tensions.

Stand with your legs slightly bent, feet about a foot apart. Ensure that there is nothing you will bump into four feet in front of you. Clasp your hands in front of you. Hold them tightly together, as if you were holding an axe between your hands. Raise your arms forward and inhale a deep breath as you do it. Immediately exhale and lower your arms between your bent knees. Exhale with a strong "hah" sound, making sure you get the energy right out of your body. Do this at least three times in a row — more if you need it.

The woodchopper is an excellent release. It instantly discharges anger energy and any other tension we may be carrying, and it revitalizes us at the same time. However, you need to be a little circumspect about where you do the woodchopper. It is not quite a main street event.

3) BEAT THE PILLOW OR BAT THE BED

Using your fists or a foam bat, beat your anger out on the bed or on your living room cushions. Imagine the cushion is the person you are angry at and really let them have it, physically, mentally, and verbally. You can kneel or stand to do this.

This is best done when no one else is around. It is much better than bashing your toes or fists on cars, fridges, and doors.

4) PUNCHING BAG OR BLOW-UP FIGURE

This serves much the same purpose as "beat the pillow." However, as the figure comes back to you, you can work up an anger response and really let your fists and body go!

5) BREATHE DEEPLY

One of the things we do automatically (and take for granted) is breathe. Think what would happen if we stopped. Now think about breathing deeply. Most of us breathe very shallowly, forgetting that our whole body needs to take in air.

This deep-breathing technique is a literal lifesaver. There are three parts to it. First, fill up your belly with a big breath and push out your navel. Now, still holding your breath, breathe into your mid-section, and then up into your chest. Hold your breath as long as you can, remembering to drop your shoulders in the process. Now gradually exhale and reverse the order — begin with the chest then exhale down and out through the belly. Repeat five times.

If done on a regular basis, this breathing exercise triggers an instant relaxation response. It also gives us a greater ability to enjoy life. It is a lifesaver when you are in a panic or are about to have an anger attack. I highly recommend it!

6) OPERA

Opera is one of those quick energy changers, and it's fun. You need to do it before you think about it or else you won't do it. All it entails is that you start singing about your frustrations in operatic fashion. You don't have to have a good voice; a raspy screech will do just fine. The intent is simply to sing out your anger. After you sing the first two lines you will undoubtedly start to laugh, and so will everyone else.

7) HUMOUR

What would we do without it? Humour is a definite godsend. We need to be mindful to use humour on ourselves, not to ridicule others or point out how funny they look.

We human beings are ridiculous in our antics. If you've ever spent any time people-watching you know how funny we are. Take this opportunity to be a humour sleuth and find out what is funny in the situation you're angry about. Think of the ridiculous. Ask yourself, "If I was to look back at this incident in 10 years, what would I find funny about it?" (Don't wait 10 years, find it now!) Next go to the mirror, look at yourself, and see how funny you are. Find just one funny thing about yourself. Don't wait until later to laugh; do it now! Have a really good laugh on yourself. Just let yourself go. Humour keeps you young. It changes the energy in any situation and it allows you to gain perspective. Laughter *is* the shortest distance between friends, so why not be a friend to yourself and laugh your troubles away?

8) EXERCISE

Exercise is very important in anger management. Exercise keeps our bodies in balance. It allows us to release toxins and physical strain. It is also good for our hearts, our muscle tone, our self-esteem, and our all-around body maintenance.

If you are a Type A personality, an "on-the-go person," try doing something relaxing, like yoga or swimming, to give your body the balance it needs. Alternate this with your squash or tennis games. *Yoga* means "union" and is especially good for releasing stress. Type A's are generally driven by tension, and they need massage and more flowing activities to create body harmony.

If you are a Type B personality, a more easy-going personality, you could take on more vigorous sports. If you have the knees for it, go for a daily jog or a brisk walk. Join a local sports group. You don't have to be a professional. Most high schools host evening classes in everything from volleyball to hockey. Racquet sports would be fine for you, as would aerobic exercise. Churning up your energy is the key for you.

Walking is wonderful for everyone. All you need is a good pair of shoes and some commitment — daily exercise is one of the best preventative anger tools around.

9) CYLINDER

Imagine you have a round stainless steel cylinder, at least six inches in diameter, right in the centre of your belly. This cylinder has an eject system that allows anything that goes into it to quickly be ejected right out of the back of your body and into the imaginary garbage dump behind you. (Maybe your eject system has an escalator to the dump.) Use this imaginary cylinder the next time someone triggers you by attacking or criticizing you. Visualize their words simply going through your body and out to the dump. This way you stay centred and uncontaminated. You can even keep your sense of humour!

10) CENTRING BREATH

Close your eyes, take a couple of deep breaths, and exhale. Now breathe in and push your navel out as you inhale. Bring your navel back as you exhale. Do this a few times, just breathe in and out and extend and contract your stomach. Concentrate on this totally.

The next time you are under fire, or are afraid you will burst with anger and do something destructive, take a few centring breaths instead. You can easily do it with your eyes wide open. No one will ever know. You will stay centred and will avoid reacting.

11) RAGE LETTER

Write a letter to the person with whom you are angry. Say everything you ever wanted to say to them. Do not edit it. Write out all your anger, then destroy the letter. Do not leave it in a place where the person you are angry at can find it. Tear it up, flush it, burn it, bury it. Writing can get your feelings out, where they can do no damage. Also, writing can often put you in touch with feelings you didn't know you had. **Under no condition do you send this letter**, even when your mind tells you it would be a good idea!

12) DO SOMETHING DIFFERENT

The next time you are angry, don't do what you usually do. Instead, do something else. If you are a yeller, say nothing. If you are a runner, stay in the room. If you crumple, if your body sags with defeat, move about and stand tall. Make sure you do something different and see what happens!

13) NOTICE YOUR FEELINGS

When you are angry or feeling sorry for yourself, notice what you're feeling. Say nothing out loud. Just notice your feelings. Become aware of them. Discover where in your body you feel your anger. Is it in your gut? Your neck? Your knees? Your lower back? What does it feel like? How much energy do you now have? Stay in close contact with your feelings until they shift, and then notice what your feelings next become. Notice your state of comfort or discomfort. Notice how each feeling you have shifts, if you just allow it.

Now breathe into your anger-holding place and relax. Write your discoveries. Keep doing this exercise until you really understand your own reactions and their deeper meaning. Then make associations with your past. Ask yourself when you felt like this before, and with whom? Ask yourself if there is anything happening right now in the present that is producing such intense feelings. Are you reliving your past? You decide. If you are in the past, you can simply drop it and focus on the present. If you are in fear, focus on your breath. Think about how you are grown-up and safe now.

14) UNDERSTAND THAT YOU ARE NOT YOUR FEELINGS

Feelings are like the clouds on a bright sunny day. They come and go as long as we don't hold onto them. So let them come and go. Don't hold onto either the pleasant or the unpleasant ones.

15) INSTANT SLOGANS

The following are some very simple and effective sayings I got from my 12-step program. I have interpreted these slogans; you could adapt them for your own use or make up your own slogans and interpretations.

a) Easy does it

This is a reminder to simply take it easy, with you and everyone else too. Breathe, relax, do whatever you need to do. Be gentle with yourself in the process. Don't complicate anything. Take it easy.

b) One day at a time

This is important for those who have little patience and feel everything has to be solved instantly. We can only live life a day at a time. There is more time to come. There *is* enough time if we live in the moment. Do what you can do today. Do your very best and let go of tomorrow.

c) Live and let live

The emphasis here is on the first "live." Live your own life to the fullest and let others live theirs according to their needs. Here's a story about "live and let live." A young man went camping in the desert. He found a beautiful spot replete with water and set up his tent for the night. Not long after he was settled, he heard some noise and noticed that he was camped beside a group of whirling dervishes. He became very upset. He paced. He swore. Then he noticed an old man whose tent was also nearby. The old man was sitting in front of his tent reading. Fuming, the young man marched over to the old man and started complaining about the dervishes. The old man nodded his head in apparent understanding. "Well, how can you stand this noise? What do you do about it?" the young man asked. "I just let them whirl," was the old man's response.

d) Let go and let God

This is the most important slogan of all. If you hold onto your less desirable feelings, your desires, your wants, and your wishes, God can't enter you or work through you. If you do things the same old way you've always done them, then you'll have the same old results. Letting go is going with the flow. It's taking it easy, staying in the moment, and doing what you need to do next. Letting go means surrender. It means realizing that you don't have all of the answers, and that you are not the master. Letting go is like exhaling: it allows you to take in a fresh new breath.

Letting go is trusting that you will be looked after. Trust is a big issue for many of us, so letting go can be threatening. If you begin with your breath — just letting go of tension — you will feel a release in your body. Nothing will ever change if we hold on. Even though it's tough to do, letting go causes miracles to happen. Let go of all of it: held regrets, resentments, anger, the lot. Let go and live the difference!

e) KISS —— Keep It Simple, Sweetheart

Ah yes, if only we could remember to keep it simple in the midst of our internal storms. Well, we can! The choice is ours. That's why I keep insisting that you return to your breathing. Deep breathing is nature's healing balm: it stills the body and the mind. So breathe and keep the rest simple.

We often make mountains out of molehills. We forget to ask ourselves, "How important is this? Will I remember it in a year?" We place such lofty importance on our ideas and our own feelings. We let our ego dominate us and we run amok. So keep it simple, sweetheart. Breathe. Ask for help. Stay in the moment. And let the rest go.

f) The Serenity Prayer

I've already extolled the virtues of this prayer. I use it whenever I remember. Like a chant, I repeat it to myself when I am in danger of losing my temper, which in my case is frequently. I say it to myself when I'm standing in front of my husband, wanting to scream at him and slam the door in his face. I say it until it works, until it penetrates my rage, until it seeps through my consciousness. I say it until I remember that it's **me** I have to change.

Then I work with my breathing. I do the three-second scream. And usually I'm centred again. If I do not become centred, I combine the other anger tools and use some slogans. I keep working on myself until I really am sane because for me losing my temper is temporary insanity, and I've had more than my share of that. I truly don't want to pay the price anymore.

16) ANGER SCRIPTS

These are phrases to use when you are so triggered that you can't say anything else. Memorize these scripts. They will come in handy.

Anything else?

Use this when the other person is heaping their garbage on you and is convinced s/he is right. Just keep asking, "Is there anything else?" in your most modulated tone, and s/he'll quickly run out of steam. I remember the day my 10-year-old son started using this on me. I was dumbstruck. It works!

"Oh"

Keep repeating "oh," instead of answering. You can smile if you want, but say nothing more than "oh." Be mindful of your tone of voice. See how many ways you can say this word. Challenge yourself to pick a very pleasant tone. You might feel like a fool, but that simple word will quickly decrease hostility. Do not rescue the other person; simply say "oh."

"Tell me more"

Mean it when you say it. "Tell me more" is a sincere attempt to gather more information, to get the facts straight. You can even write them down, asking permission first. By the third asking, the other person usually feels complete.

"You may be right.
I could be more patient, thoughtful, etc."

This is very useful when someone — particularly a family member — is criticizing you. Instead of reacting, begin to understand their point of view. Use the words "may" and "could." These words imply that you *may* be agreeing with the other person even though you *may not* be.

17) SET GOALS

Set goals when you have problems. Write out your problem list and turn each one into a goal. For example:

Problem	Goal
I feel hostile at Jim.	Improve relationship with Jim.
I am nervous around my boss.	Communicate more clearly with my boss.
I feel stressed.	Take regular de-stress breaks.

The more you focus on goal solutions, the less you will live in the problems, and the more your life will reflect this choice.

18) ABOLISH THE WORD "SHOULD"

Erase the word "should" from your vocabulary. "Should" is one of those words that points the finger — either at "them" or at you. None of us need any more "shoulds" in our lives. Change the word "should" to "could"; notice how "could" gives you options and choices.

19) HIP HIP HOORAY, I'VE MADE A MIS-TAKE!

A mistake is a chance to take it again. At one time I worked in the film business. We made many "takes" on each film. I learned a valuable lesson. A mis-take is simply a missed communication, a misinterpretation. It's an opportunity to "take it again." What matters is finding the gift in the problem. When you notice yourself or someone else making a mistake, then take it again. Find the gift. Stretch your mind. Increase your tolerance. Allow yourself to enjoy mis-takes. Make them often. Use them to learn about life, and welcome them with warmth.

20) BE A "C" STUDENT

Do this purposely. The world has more than enough people determined to become "As." Find an area in your life where you can be a "C" student and then cultivate being a "C." This means you do not have to be the expert or to live up to the highest standards. Deliberately take the pressure off yourself once in a while, and be a "C" student. You will be surprised at how much you learn about yourself from this exercise!

21) FIND SOMETHING NICE

When you are angry at someone, deliberately look for something you like about them. Find something nice and concentrate on it!

22) BE LIMITLESS

Often we set limits on ourselves, like blinders. Here is your opportunity to take those limits away, to extend yourself, to do things you haven't done for yourself in a while. Do something you don't usually do. Get a massage. Go fishing. Go bowling. Treat yourself to a delicious meal. Go to the Planetarium. Hear a concert of music you never listen to. Start drawing with your non-dominant hand. Write a love letter and send it to yourself. Visualize your success, then create it! There are absolutely no limits on this one.

23) FORGIVE AND FORGET

Yes, there will be people who do us wrong, who hurt our feelings. So what? Our job is to see what part **we** played in creating the situation. Our job is not to bring ourselves more misery. Forgiving and then holding onto resentments is not forgiving. Forgive means to "for-give, to give as before." There is only one way to forgive and that is to let go and forget. It is to let go absolutely and totally, never to drag that issue out again, no matter how tempting it is.

24) GIVE YOURSELF A HUG

Wrap your arms around you and hold on. You can do this several times a day. Tell yourself how much you love you!

There you are! Tools for you to pack up and carry with you. Tools you can use anywhere, anytime. Some are band-aids — meant to be applied temporarily — until you get calm enough to try others. Some are remedies and some are lifesavers.

Have fun with these tools. Experiment. Know that you will never be at a loss again. Become an anger technician, speeding to your own rescue whenever you are needed.

Use the tools freely and indiscriminately. Practise them regularly and add to this list. Send me any tools that you know work so I can use them too.

Be bold — and mighty forces
will come to your aid.

Basil King

Chapter Eleven

Which Animal Are You?

These are the soul cages,
These are the soul cages,
Swim to the light.
Sting

Now that you have your own anger managed, it is important to look at the conflicts you can get into with others. A definition of conflict that I like is "to be, or to come into opposition." I know there have been many times I felt I was fine at managing my own anger. It was all those other people who had problems. If only they could be good conflict managers, then I would have no difficulties. I had to discover that it was my method of handling conflicts that was getting me into trouble. So in this chapter you will have an opportunity to discover how well you handle conflicts with people you are close to. The way each one of us handles arguments with friends or loved ones is a telling sign of our conflict management style.

In the next few pages you will find a brief description of the five most typical methods of managing conflict. In the following chapter I have included a model that is based on these methods. They are called 1) Retreat, 2) Power, 3) Pleasing, 4), Manipulating, and 5) Encounter.

I have used animal symbols to describe each method and lighten up the concepts. The descriptions are based on stereotypes, but sometimes we develop patterns that are identifiable. See if some of the "animal behaviours" apply to you. Enjoy your discoveries!

1) RETREAT: The Snail

Whenever a conflict appears, the snail retreats. That's because the snail believes that conflicts are dangerous. Snails feel helpless at the very mention of a conflict. They believe it is better to stay safe inside their shells rather than risk a disagreement. Snails often have a difficult time getting close to other animals because they'd rather hide inside their shells.

2) POWER: The Barracuda

Barracudas are powerful creatures. They want what they want and are determined to get it. Barracudas believe there is only winning and losing in life. When they lose they feel weak, so they will use any tactic to gain an advantage or overpower a perceived threat. Barracudas do not take **no** for an answer. They believe their way is the only way and will fight to win. They can be dangerous.

3) PLEASING: The Spaniel

Spaniels value relationships so much they will give up anything to keep them. They need to be liked. They will run in circles in order to please. Spaniels are afraid that conflicts will harm their relationships, so they give up their needs to make sure that others' needs are met. Spaniels cannot bear to displease anyone, so they have great difficulty saying no.

4) MANIPULATE: The Coyote

Coyotes are tricksters. They can assume any pose. They are great at manipulating and often use compromise as their best ruse. They promise equality but they will take their equal share first. They try to find a mutually rewarding settlement to a conflict, but this is only temporary and the game will soon begin again.

5) ENCOUNTER: The Owl

Owls are wise birds. They often stay awake all night, looking for a solution that will benefit everyone. They know that relationships don't thrive unless both parties are satisfied. They look after their own needs. They keep one eye on the big picture, and the other on the present moment. They have courage and commitment. Owls do not run from conflicts, nor do they try to use control.

The next chapter presents the conflict management model based on these styles, so be sure to read on and discover how you can use it!

Chapter Twelve

The Conflict Management Model

In the last analysis,
our only freedom
is the freedom
to discipline ourselves.
      Bernard Baruch

Every good system has a "model" and this one is no exception. I use the conflict management model as a method of practising flexibility because flexibility is **the key** to managing conflict. I've taken the five methods of handling conflict and created a composite picture of each method so that you'll be able to identify what is good about each one. You will clearly see what is good about each method, where and how it works, when it can be useful, and what its limitations are.

145

I hope you will experiment with this model and that you will practise being "different animals." Once you have developed some versatility in using this model, you'll find yourself able to handle conflicts that used to baffle you, and often you'll be automatically operating from the Encounter style as a way of life.

So, here we go.

Conflict Method Number One: RETREAT

Retreat is the "flight" approach to conflict. Think of the person who sees someone with whom s/he doesn't want to interact coming down the street. S/he quickly crosses over to the other side of the street, bows her/his head, and hurries on. People who use retreat as a conflict management style often stay away from the issues that would bring forth a conflict. They feel that conflict is dangerous, that it is hopeless to try to resolve conflicts, so they withdraw.

Retreat can be categorized as temporary or permanent. For example, if you are stuck in your own behaviour, or are locked in a point of view with someone else, then temporary retreat is a terrific idea. It gives you time to think things over. When you're having an argument with your significant other, temporary retreat gives both of you an opportunity to cool out, to use the anger tools, and to see if you're reacting rather than responding.

Permanent retreat is the divorce court approach, or the final severance from a company. Sometimes it is the best solution.

Usually termination needs to be well thought out and should be taken as a last resort.

One of the best ways of using retreat is to talk later. "Let's talk later" can be used in the midst of a telephone call when someone is yelling at you, and you know if you don't get off the phone this very instant, you're going to blow it. You can simply excuse yourself and suggest a call back. "Let's talk later" is a great save — it doesn't accuse, point fingers, or ruin the day.

We become attached to our comfort zone

When you combine "let's talk later" with an environment change, for example meeting at a nearby restaurant rather than your office, you're really making progress. We become attached to our environments. We like to sit behind our big desk in our own chair. There are times we like to stand up and talk down to someone else. We feel comfortable in our own space. However, this comfort is dangerous. Just as often, there will be negative associations in another person's mind with your very safe place.

Remember the school principal's office that we only got called down to when there was something wrong? How did you feel about the principal's office when you were a kid? What about at home? Did your parents have a "special place" to which they would take you for disciplinary measures? Can you picture it and remember your feelings when you went there? Do you have a place in your own home in which you regularly have fights, for example the bedroom? Do you have a place for handing out discipline or punishments? How about at work? Is there a specific "discipline" room? If you use such a place routinely, it is better to find another environment, one that assures neutrality.

If you discover that you expend too much angry energy at home, one of the best places to "talk later" is at McDonald's. Practically every neighbourhood has one. You can take the kids if you need to, and give them toys to play with while you sit beside one another (not across from one another; it is too confrontational) and talk. McDonald's is anonymous. No one will listen or care about what you're saying. For the price of a coffee, you can each state your feelings or opinions. You can set a time limit on yourselves. You can listen to one another and acknowledge what you heard. You can play fair, and leave the restaurant feeling heard and understood.

An environment change is great if you know you're the "fuse-blowing" type. This way, your own environment doesn't get polluted and you probably won't end up screaming or slamming doors, which you might do if you stayed at home. It's also a great plan to seek an environment change when you're having a struggle with someone at work. It's far better to go for coffee than for a drink. Drinking changes perceptions temporarily, whereas what you want in this situation is true understanding.

If you are aware that there is a special place known for creating conflict in your office, make sure you don't go there when you have some. Places act as triggers and without intending to, we start acting out "in role."

Environment changes are great because they often promote an attitude change, and this is what is important to achieve. **Your** attitude change, remember? By the way, this might be a good time to use The Serenity Prayer!

Retreat is a powerful technique when used appropriately. I've spent many a moment in the bathroom, behind a locked door, calming myself down, instead of giving away a demented piece of my mind. Taking a walk around the block, and then another, is also effective for many people.

Retreat is not good if used on a permanent basis. The longer we leave problems the more they fester and the bigger they become, even if we can't see this. The objective is to solve the problem, not put it aside. We get into serious trouble if we adopt retreat as a solution rather than as a stopgap. If you're afraid of dealing with the situation, that's okay. It is natural to have fear, but take courage and deal with the situation anyway. Having courage means going through the fear. Otherwise, it wouldn't be courageous to do so.

Use the retreat style appropriately and you have an ally. Use it inappropriately and you often have passive-aggressive behaviour (e.g. temporary retreat, followed by attack when the other is hurting or is feeling down.) That is definitely not appropriate. Use retreat and use it wisely.

Conflict Method Number Two: POWER

Power is what many of us automatically reach for when we get triggered. It's the "I'm right" approach to handling conflict. It assumes that there is one person who has the answer and knows what must be done. It's the "my way or the highway" routine.

This is an authoritarian and often rigid style of handling conflict. Is there someone you know who uses power to deal with conflicts? (And yes, it may be you.) Get a clear picture of the person in your mind so that you can assess the benefits and pitfalls.

Using power is effective because the lines of communication are very clear. You know who is in control and there is to be no insubordination! Would you agree?

The difficulty with using power is that there really is no one person alive who has the **absolute** right answer. There is simply a point of view in operation.

People who wield power usually do so by virtue of **a) position, b) size, c) charisma.**

a) Position

Power could be wielded by the CEO of a company, the chairperson of the board, or your immediate boss. The power user definitely has a position to lend them credibility. How they use it is, of course, another matter. Politicians, leaders, government officials, judges, doctors, teachers, and gang leaders all have positions of power, as does the "head of the household." It is relatively easy to be in a position of power. It's how this power is used that makes the big difference.

b) Size

Picture a bouncer at a swank nightclub. This gives you some idea of how size is equated with power. Traditionally we see people who are large in size as powerful people. We don't necessarily feel comfortable with their size, but we respect it. In the artist Rubens' paintings, large round women were the most desirable and therefore the most powerful. Large dogs with big barks are often used as watchdogs. Large houses are power status symbols.

I believe we are in transition about the size issue. Perhaps this is a result of the dramatic influencing power that the Japanese have wielded on our business power structures. It is conceivable that compact size will reign as the next symbol of human power.

c) Charisma

This is the *"je ne sais quoi"* of power. The "either-you-have-it-or-you-don't" syndrome. Our movieland "stars" have charismatic power. Our leaders often possess it, as do well-known personalities in any field. We follow charismatic people because they represent the pinnacle of success. In a sense they have done the rising to the top for all of us. We are thus free to be voyeurs, to cheer them on, to delight in their antics, and to feel their influence.

Ah, but we are a fickle bunch. As our tastes change, we dim the light on our stars and they begin to fade. Our heroes diminish and we turn our attention to the newest, brightest attractions. Charisma is definitely an asset, but for how long?

The plus side of using power is immediate and definitive. Picture a meeting run without a chairperson. Hear the cross-talk, the interruptions, and the resulting chaos. Now imagine a chairperson deftly controlling the same meeting, and you'll see what I mean. Or visualize a beautiful new ship leaving the harbour without a captain to direct it, and imagine what would happen. Obviously there is a need for power, and certain situations that demand it.

When there's an accident you definitely want someone to take charge. When you need an operation you trust the surgeon who has power. When you're in court you want your lawyer to have power. As a temporary measure, power is, well, powerful!

Power is addictive

The difficulty is that we like the feeling of power so much that we use it indiscriminately. We lose sight of ourselves as mere mortals and elevate ourselves to gods. And then we're in trouble.

We allow our egos to take over, and egos feed on self-deception. When we can separate the job from the person, when we understand that the nature of this specific job is to make decisions, but that it does not mean that we are always right, then we have a better chance of handling power. In some cultures, the moment one achieves the highest level of success in a given field, that person must step down and start all over again in a different endeavour. This is ego insurance.

Power used for power's sake limits us. We become slaves to our own egos and we can live a lonely existence. People who wield power without regard for consequences end up as barracudas — interesting to watch from a safe distance, but to be avoided in close contact.

"Power trippers" try to trip up their opponents any way they can because they see life as a state of competition and everyone as a potential foe. This is not great for the nervous system.

Power can occasionally be used as an intervention technique, or a way of reaching an immediate decision. It is great in an emergency. Otherwise, power works best when it is equally divided and shared. Some examples in the workplace are working in self-managing teams, rotating chairpeople at meetings, instituting group decisionmaking, and acknowledging diverse viewpoints.

Power is within us

We all have power. It resides **within** us; it is innate. We need to allow our own individual power to come forth so we can use our specific talents and gifts. It is vital to be in balance with our power, and to stay in harmony with the powers of others and the universe as a whole, to keep a "power perspective."

I believe that if we consciously connect with the power of the universe — call it God, Holy Spirit, The Force, Universal Consciousness, Higher Power — then we will become adept at channelling our own power and recognizing where it comes from. We will act more often in the best interests of everyone, and not out of our own egotistical desires. Our task is to nurture the divine power within us so we can express this power creatively.

Conflict Method Number Three: PLEASING

The third conflict method is called pleasing. When it's used as a coping mechanism, it's a good one. As the name implies, pleasing means "being nice," or "smoothing ruffled feathers." It's what we do when we're having a problem with someone's behaviour, or if we know that his/her close relative has just died. We don't confront them about their behaviour. We regard them with compassion and help them through this hard time. We also do this when we know someone has recently quit smoking. We wait for his/her behaviour to level out instead of confronting him/her. We compliment him/her on what s/he is doing well and ignore the rest.

Pleasing is often a self-sacrificing mode of behaviour, a style that places other people's needs first. Pleasers are relationship people. They will sacrifice their goals or needs to preserve a relationship. They believe that if a conflict continues, the relationship will suffer; keeping the relationship is their number one concern.

Being a people pleaser

Sometimes pleasers become martyrs. They may take on too much because they can't say "No," and they end up not pleasing anyone. For example, I once had a secretary, named Marilyn, whom I shared with three other people. She was a terrific secretary and an ace people pleaser. I remember one busy Friday I asked her to have an important letter ready by 2 p.m. Marilyn said, "Sure, no problem." Joe asked her to have his report ready by noon. Marilyn smiled and said, "Yes." Nancy needed a complete update on a project by 3 p.m.; Marilyn said, "Fine."

At 3 p.m. I still hadn't got my letter, Joe's report was a mess, and Nancy had a very superficial update. Each of us was frustrated with Marilyn. She was a fine secretary, a very conscientious person. Her problem was that she couldn't say "No." She wanted to please each one of us, but she couldn't handle the workload. It would have been much better if Marilyn had said "No" to one or two of us, so that we could have made alternate arrangements.

Pleasers need to become aware of their limits, and they need to say "No." This will be difficult for both the pleaser and the party who is not used to getting a "No," but you know the saying, "No pain, no gain."

If you are a pleaser, then you are good at smoothing out situations. For example when you smile at the waiter and say the meal was fine when in fact it was lousy, you're "pleasing," and avoiding responsibility. You probably won't go back to the restaurant and you haven't given the owners of the restaurant an opportunity to make changes. If this is how you deal with conflict in general, you probably are a pleaser.

There are occasions when discretion is the better part of valour. It is wise to know when to "hold them, fold them, walk away, or run," as Kenny Rogers sings it. We all need to be considerate if we're going to get along. However, if you do tend to be a pleaser and like to smooth things over, you still need to deal with the situation at hand. Otherwise, you're placing a band-aid on a sore that could become infected.

Being a pleaser definitely has advantages. People like you and don't feel threatened by you. When it comes to managing conflicts, however, pleasing is a holding style. It works temporarily, but the objective is to **resolve** the conflict!

Note: Here's a helpful tip for pleasers. When you say "No" and people have difficulty accepting it, just ask them what part of "No" they do not understand!

Conflict Method Number Four: MANIPULATE

Manipulating is something that we learn to do as babies. We cry and our mothers come to us; we smile and they beam. We say bad words when we're toddlers and they scold or isolate us. We learn to smile to get what we want or use negative behaviour to keep people away. We learn to manipulate.

Later we manipulate friends. We trade our shovels with smaller kids in return for their toy cars. We get good at it. We become teenagers and use sex to manipulate. We get married and manipulate with threats, guilt, and rage. We run businesses and use fear and guilt to manipulate. And so it goes.

It is important to understand manipulation as a conflict management style. It is so pervasive that we use it without even knowing that we are doing so. Often we call it "**making a compromise**," and you know that our lives are full of compromises. Making a compromise can be of great benefit. Many of our business dealings are based on compromises. Our union-management disputes, our strikes, and our resolutions are usually hailed as beneficial compromises.

Sometimes we make compromises and feel fine about them. Other times they are a half measure rather than a satisfying solution. We forget that a solution is supposed to feel good and work well for **both** parties.

Having hidden agendas

The main reason that our compromises don't work is because they're **manipulative**. They can have hidden agendas or unstated expectations. We play an "I'll scratch your back if you'll scratch mine, but you scratch mine longer" game.

Manipulation doesn't work because it's a win-lose game. For example, let's assume you and I decide to go to the movies together on Tuesday nights. The first Tuesday I insist that you pick the movie. The next Tuesday I pick. Then my sister comes to town and joins us and it's only fair that she picks. And then the next Tuesday there is a movie I'm dying to see — one I know you'll want to see as well, and it will be gone by Friday, so I pick again. Now, tell me, how many movies have I picked so far? How are you feeling about this?

In a compromise, there is always someone keeping score. There are hidden expectations and a tally sheet, perhaps even an invisible scorecard with **You Owe Me** written on it. This is great if you like collecting favours. It's not so good when you owe them; usually there's interest on the debt.

For example what would you want me to do to make up for the unbalanced movie situation? I may genuinely feel that you are being selfish, and our movie nights could come to an end with both of us feeling cheated. This is a by-product of some forms of compromising.

Another difficulty with using compromise is that both people may end up with less than they would have on their own. For example using the movie analogy again, let's say that when we decide to pick the movies I like to see musicals and you like mysteries. Neither of us likes what the other one does, but we made an agreement and we want to work out a compromise. We decide to alternate our choices. Each of us must now suffer through something we would prefer not to see. If we make another compromise and opt for a third choice, let's say an adventure film, we still lose out on our own preferences. We have a middle ground, but not necessarily a choice with which we're happy.

A con-promise

I look at the word "compromise" and I see com-promise, which is like con-promise — a promise that is not. Com-promise may work for a while, but eventually we want a style of negotiating that is equally beneficial for all parties. Compromise is valuable because it can help get us there, as long as we're truthful and avoid manipulation.

If you are willing, you can observe your own manipulating and can tell the other person what you're doing, whether it is using guilt or any other emotional bribery. If you can catch it, claim it, and honestly call it, then you are playing fair. This leaves the other person free to accept or reject what you offer, with no hidden agenda. When this happens you're moving out of manipulation entirely and heading into the most effective style of conflict management, which I call Encounter.

Conflict Method Number Five: ENCOUNTER

The Encounter method is the *creme de la creme* of conflict management. It is a win-win style that benefits all parties. People who use the Encounter approach highly value their own goals and those of the other person as well. They seek a solution where both parties' needs are met and where tensions and negative feelings are worked through.

Using Encounter means operating out of mutual respect. Both the relationship and the individual are valued equally. Both grow stronger by using this method as a conflict tool.

Encounter is co-creative

The Encounter approach is co-creative. It involves being pro-active. It means being an observer, seeing the big picture — the good of the group, team, or endeavour — while at the same time understanding individual needs. This can be a demanding process. When you use the Encounter approach, you are using the conflict tools. You don't ask anyone to do something you are not willing to do yourself. You are prepared to listen to both the body language and the words being expressed. You are able to respond rather than react. You keep an open mind. You recognize your own bias and state it clearly. You take responsibility for your perception of the problem. You are able to state your own needs and preferences, and are willing to understand that the needs of others are equally important. You speak of **the conflict** as the problem, not of the person as the problem. There is no blame or finger-pointing in the Encounter method. You realize you have a perspective and not the absolute truth. Using Encounter doesn't mean we don't disagree with each other. Instead, we may agree to disagree without taking shots at one another. Here's an example.

My eldest daughter yearned for a Wheaton terrier, so I bought her one for her birthday. She was very happy with the pup but a week later I noticed she was keeping it in a cage. I don't like seeing animals caged so I told her how I felt. She informed me that it was called a "crate" and was being used for toilet training. "Because dogs don't like to sleep in their own mess they quickly learn to go outside. It's a one-stop approach to toilet training," she explained. I said the newspaper by the door seemed a more humane method. I also realized that it was not my dog. My daughter had the right to train her dog differently than I would.

We each spoke our truth, we agreed to disagree, and then we went out for dinner.

We were able to express different points of view, share feelings, and keep the communication lines open. This was a big feat!

Many business groups use Encounter in a double sense when they go away to a controlled environment, usually a retreat setting, for a few days to discuss issues. They seek solutions that will benefit both the company and the employees' interests. They brainstorm ideas and work toward achieving a group consensus.

The key is flexibility

Brainstorming is a creative Encounter tool. It involves identifying a common problem, taking suggestions from everyone without judgment, evaluating the ideas, and then agreeing upon and together implementing suggested solutions. These steps are valuable guidelines in the Encounter technique. Self-managing teams and groups that use consensus in decision making are both using the Encounter approach.

In combination with Encounter you could also use the other styles of conflict management, when appropriate. Sometimes it is necessary to retreat, to please, to compromise, or to use power. When you are flexible you can bend and incorporate different ideas. You are able to change and grow.

Use the golden rule

In using the Encounter method you operate from the golden rule. You want the best for yourself and others. People who use Encounter are not perfect, but they are willing to work problems through, to admit their own shortcomings, and to acknowledge their mistakes. As they are committed to the process of resolution, they are not afraid of conflict. Instead they welcome it, knowing that the relationship, or the company, will be strengthened through this process. They see conflict as an opportunity for growth. They celebrate their own growth and they equally celebrate the growth of others.

If you use the Encounter method, you will need to listen actively, which means to listen without interrupting or making judgements. It is often helpful to use paraphrasing to ensure understanding. The language of Encounter is personal and dynamic. Each person takes responsibility for his/her own point of view with an "I feel" or "I think" statement. For example: "I feel disappointed in the response from the group. I would prefer a more detailed approach." This statement is about one person's disappointment. It doesn't blame the group. It states the feeling with responsible language. Using "I prefer" as a request for what the person would like from the group is also responsible. There is no demand or pressure, yet there is clarity and a direct request.

Use responsible language

It is **not** responsible to say, "I feel that the group is being superficial." This is an attack on the group under the guise of an "I feel" statement. There is no feeling associated with the "I feel" in this example either. To make such a statement without requesting specific action is also not responsible. It is a form of self-pity with admonishment. The hidden message is, "You make me feel bad." Using responsible language means taking responsibility for the words expressed, ensuring that they are blame-free and clear. It means asking for feedback in the same manner; for example, "Have I expressed myself clearly?" instead of, "Did you understand?"

Using a pleasant tone of voice is equally important. That means that the voice is neither loud and commanding nor timid. It is a voice that is confident yet receptive to ideas.

By using the Encounter method, communication problems really do become growth opportunities. Any negative feelings are resolved before the issue is closed. This is a highly satisfying win-win style of managing conflict. Anyone can use Encounter on a regular basis provided they are prepared to work at it. The miracle is that other people want what you have and start copying you, so they get good at it too. Then you have a relationship, an association, or a company that is using Encounter on a daily basis. What a joyous and productive environment that is to be in.

So there they are — five methods of managing conflict for you to use and discover. Try them out, play with them, use some of this and some of that. Do some cross-breeding, mix and match them, improvise, and have fun. You are in the director's chair now and you get to decide what you will use where, when, and how.

Good luck and enjoy the process.

Chapter Thirteen

Taking an Inventory

First, keep the peace within yourself.
Then you can also bring peace to others.

Thomas à Kempis

Every business needs an inventory, a black and white ledger of stock. It's a way of keeping track of assets and debits. It's a method of assessing what material you have to work with, and how well it's working. In this case the business pertains to you, dear reader, for the business **is** you.

Often inventories are done **for** us. At work they are usually called "performance appraisals," and are done for us by our immediate superior. The difficulty is that we rarely have input into the categories for which we're being appraised. It is usually someone else's ideal of what we "should" be instead of our own. I recommend a joint performance review, wherein both parties agree upon the categories and criteria used to measure progress. This encourages commitment and there are no surprises. Regular performance reviews can be helpful. We get both feedback and encouragement.

We also may get inventories done for us at home; we call those "nagging or criticizing" inventories. We would prefer to not have these done for us, and rightly so.

It **is** important for us to take our own inventory. We each need to take stock of ourselves on a regular basis so we can clearly identify our strengths and weaknesses. We need to know what we want to build in our own character, so we can create a life that clearly works for us.

Therefore, I have constructed an inventory. This is a personal inventory, one that is tailor-made for each person. It is meant to reinforce strengths, to identify areas for improvement, and then to chart progress.

EXERCISE EIGHTEEN

Go over your inventory at the end of each day. This is your opportunity to review your behaviour, to assess what you did that was good and not so good. For example perhaps you stretched the truth a little (dishonesty), maybe you were indulgent with your anger (anger management), or played the martyr (self-pity). Place a tick beside each one of these "debits" and total them up for the day.

Then look at the assets, the good things you did. Perhaps you were patient with someone at work, maybe you were able to do some personal nurturing, or you were more honest than usual. Put a tick beside each quality. Then add up this score and see how well you are doing both with assets and debits.

I do my inventory before I go to sleep, but it can be done anytime.

Here is what a two-week sample looks like:

Daily inventory for two weeks beginning _____.				
ASSETS		**DEBITS**		
	MTWThFSS MTWThFSS		MTWThFSS	MTWThFSS
Honesty		Dishonesty		
Patience		Impatience		
Tolerance		Intolerance		
Anger Management		Anger Held/Acted		
Kindness		Stinginess		
Effort at Work		Procrastination		
Risk Taking		Isolation		
Love		Criticism		
Nurturing		Busyness		
Gratitude		Resentments		
TOTAL				

The process is short and sweet. When I am doing my inventory I am honest with myself. Then I total up the score. I know exactly where I'm at by using this inventory, and I know what my specific shortcomings are and how to remedy them. All I have to do is practise the corresponding asset.

This is a simple tool and it works well. It is particularly valuable for people who have difficulty containing anger. When I first started using it I had a lot of debits in the first week. However, as a kid who never got gold stars in school, I want them now so I started applying starts on my chart.

I use one score sheet for two weeks, because that's a do-able time frame. I then transfer my scores onto a monthly chart on which I write the scores of each asset and debit. This way I have a running total for the year, which I can see at a glance.

I bought myself a package of stars, which I use on my monthly pages. You can use anything, from stars to little coloured dots, which signify progress — anything that makes this process fun and creative for you.

If you were a kid who received lots of stars in school, then this inventory may not be a good idea for you. Instead you can go dancing!

This is a simple, quick, and effective self-management inventory. Anyone can tailor-make it for their own character building, and it will show you what you need to work on. It's private and it's yours.

One caution. This is an inventory for you to use. Be careful to take **your own inventory** and not other people's. It is always tempting to tell someone else what to do, but that doesn't help you improve.

I can tell you that since doing my inventory, I have felt increasingly better about myself. As a side benefit my productivity on all levels has increased.

Creating an inventory

To create an inventory, list 10 qualities you wish to develop. Include anger management in the 10, and monitor your progress.

Used on a regular basis, this inventory will help you to see yourself clearly, to measure the gains you make, to increase your honesty, and to strengthen your self-esteem. Above all, it's a strategy to help you validate yourself on an ongoing basis.

Using a spot-check system

Another strategy you can use is the **spot-check inventory**. The spot-check inventory helps us to recognize that every time we are upset we need to check in with ourselves, and then do whatever is necessary to let go of our resentments. We don't need to take offence at others' behaviour. Even the words "to take offence" imply that we are actively taking into ourselves a hurt that we believe someone inflicted upon us. We don't have to "take" offence and create a defence. We can leave the offence alone. We can refuse to be hurt through another's spiteful comment or cruel actions. What freedom this gives us! We become transformed through our own response to anger. The spot-check inventory also assists us by letting us know when boundaries are being crossed. If our anger is triggered when someone invades our space or if we know something isn't working for us we can say so on the spot instead of allowing tension to build.

If you are unable to do the spot-check mentally, try writing about the situation. Once you do this, ask yourself what you

167

can do to create your own inner balance. Remember to take deep relaxing breaths.

I was upset at my husband the other day because he didn't give me the praise I felt I deserved for handling a potentially volatile situation. Instead of showing him how I felt he had failed me, I went to a quiet place and wrote what had happened. I discovered that I'd been feeling insecure and wanted his praise to alleviate my anxiety. Then I gave myself the praise I wanted. I patted my own back. And, recognizing that I needed some exercise to process the inner turmoil I had created, I went for a walk.

When I returned home, I was centred and eager to be with my husband. This may sound trivial, but I've discovered that it's the little things that create the most trouble. If I am careful about the details, if I deal with my reactions as they happen, they don't become resentments. That's what spot-checking does. It enables me to work on me **before** I start blaming others.

There are undoubtedly many other forms of inventories available, but I'm keeping it simple. The best inventory is the one **that works for you**, the one you'll use consistently. The secret of any success is to do the work involved and then to reap the benefits.

By the way,

Success does not come to those who wait, and it does not wait for anyone to come to it.

Anonymous

Chapter Fourteen

Attitude Maintenance

Live decently, fearlessly, joyously,
and don't forget
that in the long run,
It's not the years in your life,
but the life in your years that counts.

Anonymous

Have you ever wondered why some people who appear to have so little to be grateful for are happy, while others who have a lot are miserable? Do you think it's a cosmic joke?

I know one thing. No matter what is going on around us, how much pain or physical discomfort we're in, how difficult our present situation is, we can control our reactions by maintaining our attitude.

Last year my mother-in-law had two hip operations and discovered that she had throat cancer as well. She went through surgery, had radiation treatments, and spent six months eating only soft porridge. Yet she greeted each day with a positive attitude. Her actions reinforced this attitude.

Her special talents were knitting and baking. She kept herself feeling positive by concentrating on what she could give to others. In hospital she got right to work, knitting sweaters, socks, and hats for everyone she could think of. When she returned home, she baked. The postman regularly received cookies. The grocery store manager got a pie. Her priest got weekly care packages. Everyone in her family received her bounty. She had a lilt in her limp, a twinkle in her eye, and she kept herself happy with attitude maintenance.

My friend Liane was told she had incurable bowel cancer and that she had six months to live. Liane went to a self-healing institute and took workshops. She found a doctor who was also a naturopath and who specialized in the immune system. Liane took vitamins, exercised daily, and did a lot of work on forgiveness. She screamed her anger out. She beat the mattress until she was exhausted. She danced. She bought herself a puppy. She learned meditation and visualization. Six months passed. A year passed. Liane's health is now improving, but even if it wasn't, she would be okay. She realized that it's not *how long* she has to live, it's *how* she lives that counts.

There's a fellow I know who has a major heart condition and emphysema. Every day he seems thinner, more frail. His smile is always ready, and his standard line is "How sweet life is." He is not pretending. He is grateful for each moment he has.

Why is it that some of us don't appreciate what we have until it's gone? I think it's because l) we take life for granted, and 2) we haven't practised being grateful.

Anyone, anywhere, can become grateful. All it takes is awareness. You can start with a gratitude list. That's a list of things to be grateful for, and you can start with the simplest ones, like l) you're alive and 2) you can read this book. You can start with two things if that's all you can find. Go over your gratitude list at night before retiring and in the morning upon awakening. Do this every day for a week and note the difference it makes in your attitude.

Develop the gratitude habit

If you are having difficulty with your mate, make a list of the qualities you appreciate about him/her. Then tell your mate two or three of these every day. Say "I appreciate the fact that you're so _____." Get into the appreciation habit and watch it grow.

If you feel down on yourself, go to the mirror and spend two minutes looking into your own eyes, telling yourself you love and accept yourself just the way you are. It's okay if you don't believe it at first. Say it over and over again every day and eventually you **will** believe it.

Order my tapes on "Celebrating Anger" or "Self-Talk Your Way to Success" and listen to them regularly. Read nurturing books. At the end of this book I have included a bibliography of books that I have read and found helpful. You can find them at your local book store. Buy tapes and videos that affirm your best choices. Do what they suggest. Reward yourself with praise.

By the way, these exercises are not meant to suggest you wear a false smile or twist yourself into a pretzel. They are meant as suggestions to help you discover your own inner gratitude.

There is so much good material available waiting for you. Inspiration exists on every street; you just have to notice it.

An attitude of gratitude needs to be cultivated. If you don't take the weeds out of your garden, they'll strangle your flowers. The same is true of inner gardening. You need to plant the seed of gratitude and then tend it. Water this garden, uproot the weeds of discontent, and enjoy your harvest.

Chapter Fifteen

The Last Word

Commit random kindness and
senseless acts of beauty.

Sara Steele

Well, here we are at the end of this book. You have the understanding now, the anger tool kit, the model, and the information. Now it's up to you.

Don't be afraid. You can do it. I know you can. Begin where you are, right now. Begin with just one thing. Remember, every journey starts with the first step.

So start stepping!

I want you to know that I loved writing this book for you. Of course, I wrote it for me as much as for you, but I kept your faces in my mind as I was writing: faces of those of you I've met already, and those of you I haven't yet met personally but I know are there. Do this wonderful anger work and do it with a light heart. Let me know what your discoveries are. I will be delighted to hear from you.

There is simply no substitute for doing the work. Believe me, I've tried. If you don't want to do it, at least acknowledge that for today you are choosing not to do the work and are willing to accept the consequences of your actions.

Practise living **one day at a time**. When you do this you can deal with anything, any loss or any gain. You can accept your anger or your sadness for just one day, and that's all any of us ever really has. Know that what you feel now will pass. Remember you always have options.

Most important, develop faith in a power greater than yourself. This is the power that will see you through and give you true security. Realize that you are not the master of the universe. There **is** something out there you can rely on, something that created the vastness you see every day. You don't have to be perfect, your job is just to be YOU.

Realize that what you do have is choice. It is always up to you to choose how you want to act or react. If you want quality of life, then you need to create it. If you want to celebrate your anger, to experience your passion, to feel your aliveness, you need to acknowledge your feelings as they arise, without masking them or making them nice or wrong.

Don't be afraid of your own anger. Remember anger just shows you that there is some area in you to release or investigate. When you use your anger this way, it becomes your friend. It won't hurt you; it will give you freedom.

Use the anger tools to take charge of how you express your anger. Repeat The Serenity Prayer. Create a balanced lifestyle and, most importantly, appreciate yourself every single day of your life.

Make friends with your own little inner Child.

Hug and heal that wounded one.

Become your own nurturing parent.

Allow your inner little boy to make mistakes.

Tell that inner little girl that you won't abandon her again.

Uncover your uniqueness.

Express your creativity.

Enjoy being you.

Laugh regularly.

Laughter is inner jogging.

Norman Cousins

Allow yourself to laugh more. Say "ha ha ha ha" over and over again until you start to laugh at nothing. Read the comics. See funny movies. Go to the airport and watch the brilliant parade of people. Notice how funny we all are, including yourself, especially when you are angry. See the delightful absurdity in everything. Look for the gift in each problem and you will find it.

Love yourself for being exactly the way you are. There is no one else like you, no one with your gifts. You are the only you that ever was or ever will be. You are precious. When the special radiance of your light shines in the world, the universe rejoices.

Treasure the treasure that you are.

Give to yourself. Give to others.

Remember:

People don't care about how much you know, it's how much you care that counts.

Angela Jackson

Celebrate yourself!

I celebrate you with you.

Notes

Notes

Notes

BIBLIOGRAPHY AND RECOMMENDED READING

In the presence of a Master-Gurudev, Yogi Amrit Desai. Lenox, Kripalu, 1992.

Beattie, Melody. *Beyond Co-Dependency.* Minn: Hazeldon Foundation, 1989.

Berne, Eric. *Games People Play.* New York: Random House, 1964.

Bly, Robert. *Iron John.* New York: Addison-Wesley, 1990.

Bradshaw, John. *Homecoming.* New York: Bantam, 1990.

Campbell, Giraud W. *A Doctor's Proven New Home Cure for Arthritis.* West Nyack: Bantam, 1972.

Eyton, Audrey. *The F-Plan Diet.* New York: Bantam, 1982.

Hay, Louise L. *You Can Heal Yourself.* Santa Monica: Hay House, 1984.

Hausman, Patricia & Hurley, Judith Benn. *The Healing Foods.* New York: Dell, 1989.

Hendrix, Harville. *Getting The Love You Want.* New York: Holt, 1988.

Katzen, Mollie. *Moosewood Cookbook.* Berkeley: Ten Speed Press, 1977.

Keen, Sam. *Fire in the Belly.* New York: Bantam, 1991.

Kravette, Steve. *Complete Meditation.* Pennsylvania: Whitford Press, 1982.

Kushi, Aveline and Esko, Wendy. *The Changing Seasons Macrobiotic Cookbook.* New Jersey: Avery, 1985.

Mandino, Og. *The Choice.* New York: Bantam, 1984.

Jampolsky, Gerald. *Teach Only Love.* New York: Bantam, 1983.

Peck, M Scott. *The Road Less Travelled.* New York: Simon & Schuster, 1978.

Siegal, Bernie S. *Love, Medicine and Miracles.* New York: Harper & Row, 1986.

ABOUT THE AUTHOR

ANGELA JACKSON is a professional speaker who comes from the heart. Her powerful message moves audiences. Her varied working background in education, counselling, and business enables her to bring depth and diversity to her seminars.

A graduate of both York University and the University of Toronto, Angela has motivated organizations, corporations, and associations throughout North America. She is committed to making a difference in how people relate and to inspiring individuals to reach past their barriers and take a positive stand in life.

The mother of three grown children, she resides in Toronto, Canada, with her husband and two cats.

TO THE MEETING PLANNER

If you are responsible for securing speakers for your conferences, conventions, and special events, you'll want to explore the many benefits of bringing Angela Jackson to your group. She is a dedicated and committed professional who will design every program to meet the specific needs of your audience. Here are some testimonials about her programs.

"This was an excellent, heart-warming presentation, filled with practical ideas and insight." **Rebel Hardy, Account Manager, Humber College**.

"A jam-packed information session. The pace never slowed and Angela's enthusiasm never waned. Thoroughly enjoyed every minute and learned a lot." **Doug Evans, Vice President, Marketing, The Arrow Company**.

"Thank you for presenting "Conflict Management for Everyone" at our National Conference. Not only was the topic timely, but by involving the audience, it gave more meaning to the session and drove your message home. People enjoyed the session more because of your own enthusiastic manner in presenting your material and your use of personal examples to emphasize a point. A valuable and most enjoyable session." **Linda Martin, Meeting Planner, Canadian Automotive Electric Association**.

ANGELA JACKSON can help you be successful at your next event. Call, write, or fax for information about the following keynote presentations or seminars:

- CELEBRATING ANGER - *Creative Solutions for Managing Conflict*

- FROM FRAZZLE TO DAZZLE - *Success in Stress Management*

- ARE YOU LISTENING? - *The Art of Communicating*

- TEAM EXCELLENCE - *Together Everyone Achieves More*

- THE POWER OF CHOICE - *Success Strategies for the '90s*

- PUTTING ON THE RITZ - *How to Give Superb Customer Service*

- CREATIVITY IN THE WORKPLACE

- ENHANCING SELF-ESTEEM

ANGELA JACKSON & ASSOCIATES
2693 Lakeshore Blvd. West, Suite ll,
Toronto, Ontario, Canada
M8V lG6
Tel: (4l6) 259-3365 Fax: (4l6) 255-6627

Would someone you know benefit from reading *Celebrating Anger?* This is a perfect gift for a family member or friend who has difficulty handling anger, a colleague who is either storing or exploding with anger, the executive who needs fresh ideas to inspire people, or a couple who have difficulty communicating.

Please send me _____ copies of *Celebrating Anger*.

I have enclosed a cheque made payable to **Angela Jackson & Associates** for $15.00 + $2.50 (tax, shipping and handling) each in the amount of _____ copies x $17.50 = $ _____ .

Name: _____

Address: _____

City: _____ Province (State): _____

Postal (Zip) Code: _____ Telephone: (____) _____

SEND ORDERS TO:
Angela Jackson & Associates,
2693 Lakeshore Blvd. West, Suite ll,
Toronto, Ontario, Canada M8V lG6
Tel: (4l6) 259-3365 Fax: (4l6) 255-6627

☐ Please send autographed copies.

☐ Please inscribe the book(s) with this message:

_____

_____

* There is a discount for large orders.

25 copies or more - 10%

100 copies or more - 20%

500 copies or more - 30%

(Please allow four to six weeks for delivery.)

Would someone you know benefit from reading *Celebrating Anger*? This is a perfect gift for a family member or friend who has difficulty handling anger, a colleague who is either storing or exploding with anger, the executive who needs fresh ideas to inspire people, or a couple who have difficulty communicating.

Please send me _____ copies of *Celebrating Anger*.

I have enclosed a cheque made payable to **Angela Jackson & Associates** for $15.00 + $2.50 (tax, shipping and handling) each in the amount of _____ copies x $17.50 = $ _____.

Name: _____

Address: _____

City: _____ Province (State): _____

Postal (Zip) Code: _____ Telephone: (____)_____

SEND ORDERS TO:
Angela Jackson & Associates,
2693 Lakeshore Blvd. West, Suite 11,
Toronto, Ontario, Canada M8V 1G6
Tel: (416) 259-3365 Fax: (416) 255-6627

☐ Please send autographed copies.

☐ Please inscribe the book(s) with this message:

_____

_____

* There is a discount for large orders.

25 copies or more - 10%

100 copies or more - 20%

500 copies or more - 30%

(Please allow four to six weeks for delivery.)

DO YOU NEED HELP HANDLING CONFLICT?

Help is but a telephone call or fax away. Call us, or fax or mail this page to the address below, and you will be contacted as soon as possible.

Yes, I have read *Celebrating Anger* and would like help. (please check)

- ☐ There are communication problems with my staff.
- ☐ I need help motivating my people.
- ☐ There is a lot of conflict on the job.
- ☐ We are under a lot of stress and need education and techniques.
- ☐ We need teamwork training.
- ☐ Help me motivate my sales group.
- ☐ We have some difficult people at work. Help me handle them.
- ☐ Help me use the tools in your book.
- ☐ We need superior customer service training.
- ☐ Help me empower my staff.
- ☐ We have difficulties with self-esteem issues.
- ☐ We need assistance in creating a wellness program.
- ☐ Help us get more creative.
- ☐ We need anger counselling.
- ☐ We want to purchase more books at a volume discount.

☐   Other, please describe: _____

_____

_____

Name: _____

Title: _____

Organization: _____

Address: _____

City: _____

Province/State: _____

Postal or Zip Code: _____

Telephone No.: _____

Fax No.: _____

Mail to: Angela Jackson & Associates
           2693 Lakeshore Blvd West, Suite ll
           Toronto, Ontario, Canada M8V lG6
           Tel. (4l6) 259-3365 or Fax (4l6) 255-4635